Heavenly Realm Publishing
Houston, Texas

Position Your *Faith* for Great *Success*

VOLUME 1

A guide to help you heal from the pain of your past, and release God's faith and favor to fulfill the purpose that He has placed on your life.

EACH CHAPTER OFFERS A POWERFUL 7 DAY SERIES OF STUDY AND FAST TO PUSH YOU TOWARDS YOUR PURPOSE IN LIFE

I encourage and challenge you to purchase the, "Position Your Faith for Great Success Workbook". It is filled with faith scriptures, declarations, confirmations, bible quizzes; questions and answers on faith, success, purpose, and promise.

WARNING:

The fasts suggested in this book are not for everyone. Consult your physician or your Pastor before beginning the suggested fasts at the end of each chapter if you are uncertain about your health or have a history of health problems, or spiritual breakdowns. It is not God's will to hurt, harm, physically, or emotionally harm anyone's body through these physical, spiritual exercises. It is my heart's desire as the author of this book to motivate, encourage, and to help each person who reads this book to grow and receive everything that God has promised as you walk up your ladder of purpose.

> "... behold a ladder set up on the earth, and the top of it reached to heaven: and behold the angels of God ascending and descending on it.
> And, behold, the LORD stood above it, and said, I [am] the LORD God of Abraham thy father, and the God of Isaac: the land whereon thou liest, to thee will I give it, and to thy seed;
> And thy seed shall be as the dust of the earth, and thou shalt spread abroad to the west, and to the east, and to the north, and to the south: and in thee and in thy seed shall all the families of the earth be blessed.
> And, behold, I [am] with thee, and will keep thee in all [places] whither thou goest, and will bring thee again into this land; for I will not leave thee, until I have done [that] which I have spoken to thee of."
>
> *Genesis 28:12-15 kjv*

Your future is on the ladder. Your purpose is on the ladder. Your blessings are ascending and descending up and down the ladder until you reach the top. Do not get tired. Do not give up. Do not give in. Do not get off of the ladder until your assignment is completed. Your blessings are right in front of you. Do you receive it? If so, you are now ready to begin reading this book. It will literally change your perspective of how you perceive life, faith, future, and your purpose.

—Stephanie Franklin

FAILURE IS NOT YOUR FINAL DESTINATION, DELAY IS NOT DENILE.

You have the faith and the power to reach the unreachable, to do the impossible, out think the unthinkable, and see what has never been seen before...

—Stephanie Franklin

*Enjoy your life where you are and do not worry
about your tomorrow.
God will take care of your tomorrow.*

~Stephanie Franklin~

THE FOUNDATION IS ALREADY LAID.
JUST BELIEVE, OBEY, AND RECIEVE.

~Stephanie Franklin~

This book of the law shall not depart out of thy mouth; but thou shalt meditate therein day and night, that thou mayest observe to do according to all that is written therein: for then thou shalt make thy way prosperous, and then thou shalt have good <u>success</u>.

Joshua 1:8, kjv

Many are the plans in a man's heart, but it is the Lord's purpose that prevails.

Proverbs 19:21

Also By Stephanie Franklin

When Ramona Got Her Groove Back from God
My Song of Solomon
My Song of Solomon *Prayer Journal*
Position Your *Faith* for Great *Success* Workbook

Position Your *Faith* For Great *Success*

Stephanie Franklin

Heavenly Realm Publishing
Houston, Texas

Unless otherwise indicated, all scriptures quotations in this book are from the Holy Bible King James Version, Amplified, and NIV version.

Copyright © 2010 *by* Stephanie Franklin.
All rights reserved.

Copyright © 2010 Position Your Faith for Great Success.
Volume 1. *by* Stephanie Franklin
All rights reserved.

Cover Illustration and Design © 2010, *by*
Heavenly Realm Publishing.
All rights reserved.

ISBN—13: 978-0-9825589-3-5

Library of Congress Control Number: 2010929013

This book is printed on acid free paper.

Printed in the United States of America

No part of this book may be reproduced, stored in a retrieval system, or transmitted by any means, electronic, mechanical, photocopying, recording, or otherwise, without written permission from the author.

**Published By: Heavenly Realm Publishing Company
505 N. Sam Houston Pkwy. E., Suite 670, Houston, Texas 77060,
toll free 1-877-599-3237.**

I first dedicate this book to my best friend in Heaven and on the earth, my Father, I Am—God.

I second dedicate this book to my family and best friend, you all know who you are….. I love you for loving me and pushing me to great success and purpose.

Contents

Position Your *Faith* for Great *Success,* VOLUME 1

The Introduction
The Preface

Faith Session 1

Birthing Your Purpose from Your Pain   **57**
Hell Faith to Heaven Faith   **77**
Faith as Easy as Saying 1, 2, 3   **93**
Prosperity Come to me Right Now!   **113**
Don't Panic, it's Only a Test   **129**
It's a Set Up   **149**

Faith Session 2

Iron Sharpens Iron   **169**
Two Heads Are Better Than One   **191**
You Are Special Like the Cedar Tree   **207**
Don't Judge A Book by its Cover   **227**
The Potter and the Clay   **245**
I'm All That God Say's I Am   **263**

Faith Session 3

Can These Dry Bones Resurrect and Live?   **279**
When My Bones Became Flesh through Faith   **293**
Turn Your Water into Wine   **309**
When the Devil Steals Your Word of Faith   **323**
When the Lord Calls Your Name say, "Here I am."   **337**

Faith Session 4

You Shall Have What You Speak   **359**
The Foundation Is Already Laid   **377**
It's Your Appointed Season   **401**
Stay Close to the Vine   **419**

Spiritual Blessings in Christ

For He foreordained us (destined us, planned in love for us) to be adopted (revealed) as His own children through Jesus Christ, in accordance with the purpose of His will.

(So that we might be) to the praise and commendation of His glorious grace (favor and mercy), which He so freely bestowed on us in the Beloved.

In Him we have redemption (deliverance and salvation) through His blood, the remission (forgiveness) of our offenses (shortcomings and trespasses), in accordance with the riches and generosity of His gracious favor.

Which He lavished upon us in every kind of wisdom and understanding (practical insight and prudence).

Making known to us the mystery (secret) of His will (of His plan, of His purpose). [And it is this:] In accordance with His good pleasure (His merciful intention) which He had previously purposed and set forth in Him.

In Him we also were made (God's) heritage (portion) and we obtain an inheritance; for we had been foreordained (chosen and appointed beforehand) in accordance with His purpose, who works out everything in agreement with the counsel and design of His [own] will.

Ephesians 1:5-9, 11 –amplified

YOU'RE PRAYER CONFESSION OF FAITH FOR YOUR JOURNEY AS YOU READ AND STUDY EVERY CHAPTER

Lord, I thank You for dying on cross just for me. I thank You for choosing me to read and to study this book in a way that will help me heal from the pain of my past, and reposition my faith to have great success in my future. I declare and believe that I can and I will have great success in my future.

I thank You that I have the power to over-come every obstacle and every challenge in order to fulfill my purpose in life.

Lord, I thank You for granting me favor and for putting me in position to do and to receive the impossible, to reach the unreachable, to out think the unthinkable, and to go to places that no man has gone before.

I declare and decree that my life is a living example for my posterity and for my family.

I declare and decree that as I sow my seed, my seed comes back to me in good measure, pressed down, shaken together, and running over, and that men shall give into my bosom.

I thank You that I have more than enough, and there is no lack in my life, my finances, my spiritual walk, and in my purpose and destiny….. Amen.

A PRAYER CONFESSION OF FAITH FOR EACH DAY OF THE WEEK

Verbally speak this prayer confession in faith everyday before you start your day. Pin it up on your mirror, in the bathroom, on your wall, in your car, or where ever you need to, and watch God bless each day for you.

MONDAY:

Lord, I thank You that You have gone before me and have prepared my day. I thank You that You have filled my day with joy, love, peace, protection, and with the power to make a difference in someone's life…. Amen.

TUESDAY:

Lord, I thank You for allowing me to see another day. I thank You for going before me and for preparing my day. I thank You for filling my day with favor, love, peace of mind, and for giving me prosperity from unexpected places. I thank You for the power and strength to make it through this day and to make a difference in someone's life….Amen

WEDNESDAY:

Lord, I thank You for blessing this mid—day of the week. I thank You that You have blessed Monday and Tuesday, and that You have already gone before me and have given me the victory over every obstacle that may come my way. I thank

You for the power to make a difference in someone's life on today….Amen

THURSDAY:

Lord, I thank You that You have gone before me and have prepared my day. I thank You for the ability to win and not to loose. I thank You that according to Luke 6:38 that as I give, more shall be given back to me in good measure, pressed down, shaken together, and running over shall men give into my bosom. Thank You for the power to reach and to win a soul on today….Amen

FRIDAY:

Lord, I thank You for going before me and for preparing my day. I thank You that everything that I do, places I go, whom I come in contact with, and what You have prepared for me, lines up with Your word and with Your will for my life. Thank You for the power to make a difference in someone's life on today….Amen

SATURDAY:

Lord, I thank You for preparing my day on today. I thank You that no worries will be a part of this day, and I thank You that the devil is defeated and I move another step closer to my purpose and destiny. Thank You that today will be a blessed day for me….Amen

SUNDAY:

Lord, thank You because this is the day that You have made and I will rejoice and be glad in it! I thank You for going before me and for preparing this day, and that it will be full of rejoicing and full of praise! I decree and declare that I will bless You at all times and Your praises shall forever be in my mouth. Thank You that I rest in Your love and close out this week victoriously! Thank You for allowing me to release everything that may have hindered my peace, and has kept me from drawing closer to You from this week; and I thank You that I am able to start fresh on next week with great success….Amen

Position Your *Faith*

Faith:

Faith is the sounding board to God's heart. It is merely what moves God to do the impossible.

for Great *Success*

Success:

Great success is not determined by the pain of your past, it is determined by how you overcome it.

Future

Future is the road that God uses to complete the mission that He has placed on your life to do the impossible, to reach the unreachable, to conquer what has never been conquered before; the road to your mission and destiny of why you were ever created—your purpose.

Acknowledgements

First and foremost all of my acknowledgments and thank you's belong to You Lord. You are my best friend; not because You are unchangeable, but because of who You are in my life, and what You mean to me in my heart. You are just that amazing!

I would like to acknowledge and thank my entire family and friends. I love you all for just being who you are. I have learned that there is not one family that is without blemish. Thank you for being real. God is going to bless all of us real good. I decree and declare the purpose and the blessings of God on each and every one of your lives.

The Introduction

I want to start by saying it ain't over until God says it's over. Your latter days will be greater than your past. It would be easy for anybody who sees you right now in your current situation to look at the struggles that you are going through in your life and say, "it's over for you. You'll never have great success, you'll never win. You'll never amount to anything. You're not about nothing. You're a disgrace. I'm glad they hurt you, you deserve what happened to you. God won't use you, look at your past..." Don't listen to them. Those are words from the devil and as long as you're trusting in God, you'll never be defeated. You will always win. I want you to know that God is ready to position your faith, your life, your career, and your future for great success! Go after it! Get the best out of every opportunity that God gives you! This is your season and no devil, no hater, no past issues, can stop it!

In order to have great success, you must first have the faith to believe that God can and will make your life great, and give you the ability to obtain great success. Nothing will just come to you, you have to position yourself, your faith, your mind, your mouth, your actions, your attitude, your career, your abilities; and your entire life and get out there and go after it. Now the key word is, POSITION. You must position your faith—get in the place to receive. For example, if you want to own your own business. To position yourself, you have to first seek God for the vision. Then you have to do the necessary things in the natural, meaning in the physical. You must write the vision down as He gives it to you. Then you have to seek God on WHERE HE HAS CHOSEN YOUR PLACE OF BUSINESS TO BE LOCATED. Nothing is chosen by you. Only God can choose your place (career, business, church, home, job, finances, etc.) You have to be careful NOT TO CHOOSE THE PLACE YOURSELF. Only God knows what's best and He is the reason why you thought of the vision in the first place. He has a purpose for the vision that He gave you. Purpose does not come for you, it comes for the purpose of God getting the glory in it. There is something that God wants to do with the vision that He has given to you. You have to get out there and acquire the place for your business. You have to go and look at different properties (lands), buildings, etc. Do not worry about how much it cost, or how big it is, God will do the impossible. God will always show you something that seems impossible, because if it was possible and looked like the ordinary, He would not get the glory and everybody would be doing it or have it. Once you acquire the place, now you're in position. You've just crossed over to receive. You may say, "But I don't have the money. Or this is crazy, this is way out of my league, that building is much too large. That land is too many acres—my little vision can't handle that. My boss will never give me that raise—that amount of money." If you have that kind of faith, you're not in position. To know that you are in position is to be in that place even though it looks impossible, you're standing on the word of God, confessing that your vision will come to pass, pinning up drawings concerning your vision on a wall and prophesying to them daily, and last waiting on God to move. Now let me tell you how He'll do the impossible. He'll do it just when you're not expecting it. He'll send someone or open the channels of blessing through an open position or source and have that land available for you. The impossible would be that the owner of the land would come along and say you can have the 3.5 acres of land for FREE. This is how God will do it and more. The fact that you are now in position, this puts God in a MUST MOVE POSITION. After you've done all that you know to do to stand according to the word of God, then just stand and wait on the MUST MOVE OF GOD. It's on Him now and trust me, He will not let you down.

I realize believing for great success can be a very hard thing to do, especially when you had no faith in the very beginning, or you just didn't know how to have faith. I'm sure there are some that are asking, "what do you mean I didn't have any faith?" Well, simple, what I mean is that in the past you may have been going through a challenging situation where you thought you were going to loose your mind, and faith was the last thing on your mind. All you were thinking about was how you were going to get *yourself* out it, instead of thinking how *God* was going to get you out of it. Faith is not how you're going to do it, faith is how God is going to do it.

Although God gives you the ability and the tools to do it yourself, the source still comes from Him and not from you. *[Hebrews 11:6]* You must have faith.

You may say that you have faith and believe that God will answer your prayers and change your situation around but you <u>doubt</u> when He gives you instruction or the answer to your prayers. For example, when Jesus directed the disciples to get on a ship they had to get on, the storm began to rage and it seemed as if the ship was going to turn over, the disciples began to panic, that was <u>doubt</u>. Suddenly they saw Jesus walking on the water. They were so afraid <u>and did not believe</u> that it was really Jesus and the bible says that they thought it was a spirit. Peter shouted and said, *"Jesus if it's really you, bid me to come to you on the water."* Jesus gave him the heads up, meaning he said come on, and Peter began to walk out on the water by faith, <u>and as long as he was believing, he was making progress</u> and on his way towards getting closer to Jesus *[to great success]*, but the bible says that Peter began to fear (he began to doubt) and then he began to sink and faithlessly [doubt] he called out to Jesus to help him and Jesus immediately stretched forth his hand and saved him; and then said, *"ye' of little faith, why do you <u>doubt</u>?"* I'm sure Peter was without words after that question. This is what I mean by not having any faith in God. God has already given to us faith. But He has given it to us in such a way that we realize that we cannot possibly make it without Him nor can we nearly walk on water by ourselves, let-alone try to figure out the answer to our life's problems, situations, and dilemmas. *[Matthew 14:22-33]* Another example is when you had to go to the doctor for something minor and when you got in there, the doctor said that you only had a few months to live; or the doctor diagnosed you with an incurable disease. You came out saying, "I'm a dead person now", instead of believing what the word says in *[Isaiah 53:5]* about God being *"…wounded for your transgressions, he was bruised for your iniquities; the chastisement of your peace was upon him; and <u>**with his stripes you are healed**</u>"*. Jesus came to this earth for this very thing. He took your sickness and made it His when he died on the cross for your sins. The bible says that *"he was wounded for your transgressions"*. Jesus went through all of that pain just for you to have the faith to believe that by all of those stripes, all of those scares, cuts, and deep bruises on his body, you <u>were</u> already <u>healed</u> because he already took the pain for you. Notice I said the word, "were" in the sentence above? This is not an error, I meant to say were—in past tense, because by faith you are already healed because Jesus came and died just for that sickness or disease that seems unbearably incurable in your life right now. He's already wiped it all away all He's waiting for, is for you to believe His word and not the report of the doctor. Make sense? Hope so.

Having faith can be very difficult at times especially when you cannot see how God is going to work your situation out. But when you've done all that you can to stand, just stand. My life was like a roller coaster ride as I first began walking up this tall ladder called life. It was a roller coaster ride when I didn't know the Lord, didn't know who I was in Him, and how to have faith to believe for the supernatural. When I realized how special I was to God, I began to gain confidence in the truth that God made me a beautiful creature. His will for my life has taken care of me, and His will is still taking care of me right now. I had very little knowledge of who the Lord was in my early young adult life that I turned and went into directions that the Lord had not directed me too. I hung around some people that I should not have been hanging around, which drove me up and down and around like a roller coaster ride. God has purposed our lives like climbing up a tall ladder. I want you to visualize how a five hundred foot tall ladder looks while you are standing at the bottom and trying to look up. Trying to see the top is very hard isn't it? This is our very own lives. Even though we cannot see our end, we know it's victorious because the ladder belongs to the Lord and He is the One who determines how high your ladder is; and whether or not you're ready to go up to the next step. Before you can go up to the **next step**, you have to be tried and tested. Once you pass the test[s], then you're strong enough to go up to the **next step**. If you fail the test[s], you will have to keep taking the same test[s] over and over again until you pass it/them. Then you can go up to the **next step**. You notice that I said, <u>go up</u> to the **next step**? Yes, your life is going up as long as you are going up. This means you are living according to God's word, trusting; and relying on Him in everything that you say and do. The bible says, to *"trust in the Lord with all your heart, and lean not unto your own understanding, [6] in all your ways acknowledge him, and he shall direct your path." [Proverbs 3:5-6]*. You must trust God no matter what, even if you can not possibly see how He's going to work the situation out, or how He's going to possibly heal your body, or how He's going to turn your finances around, or how He's going to deliver your husband or wife, or how He's going to find you a job, or how He's going to remove the depression you've been dealing with all of your life, or how He's going to help you to forgive those who have hurt you in the past, or how He's going to help you with gluttony because you can't stop over eating and gaining weight, or, or, or, and the list goes on. You must trust Him to do it anyway. Remember I just shared the story from the bible where Peter came out of the ship and proceeded to walk on the water towards Jesus until he became afraid and began to sink? Well, this is what happens when we become afraid and stop trusting God in every area of our lives; we start to sink just like Peter did. But the good news is, if this fits you, Jesus is standing right in front of you as you repent and call out to Him for help, He will immediately as the bible says, He *"...will immediately stretch out his hand and save you"*. He will help you in all of those areas that you are struggling in and will begin to change your life forever.

You have to find out who you are now that you're here on this earth.

The Preface

What ever you are believing God for, it will come to past; *"as He has purposed, so shall it stand. The purpose that God has purposed on your life, with His omnipotent hand is stretched out all over the nation. For the Lord of many hosts has purposed, who can annul it? His hand is stretched out, and who can turn it back?"* [Isaiah 14:24-27] The answer to these questions are simple, no one can stop or turn back the purpose that God has placed on your life. This is the reason why you were created before you were even in your mother's womb. This is why He says that *"…he formed you even before you were in your mother's womb."* [Jeremiah 1:5] So this is not an option to ever give up or to give in.

As you read this book and study the short 7—Day Series of Study at the end of each chapter, I challenge you to position your faith for great success. Drop all of the pain you have gone through, how you can't get over the hurts, the wounds, the scares of your past, why he or she left you, the fact that you feel so ugly and fat, and you can't see why God would create you to fulfill any kind of purpose; whose fault it has been as to the reason why you have not done what God has called you to do for years, and the fear that keeps you from fulfilling the purpose that God has placed on your life to complete.

All of these statements and questions will continue to run through your mind until you release them and move on towards your purpose.

This book has a <u>Workbook</u> that is sold with it entitled: "Position Your Faith for Great Success *Workbook*". You do not want to miss purchasing this Workbook. It is packed with a complete 7-day series of study, 7-day fast, daily promise, daily devotion, bible reading for morning and evening, bible quizzes, day by day grace revelations, faith scriptures, declarations, confession of faith's, questions and answers on faith, success, purpose, and promise. I encourage and challenge you to purchase the Workbook it will draw you that much closer to great success.

1

Birthing Your Purpose From the Pain of Your Past

Faith Session 1

Birthing Your Purpose From the Pain of Your Past

The thought of shouts coming from a woman in excruciating pain from labor can be very intense and painful, even if you're not the one in labor. If you're not a woman or have never had a baby, think of a time when you had to endure a very painful moment in your life. Maybe you broke your arm or leg. Maybe you lost a loved one, or maybe you had sickness in your body, maybe your husband or wife left you, or maybe you've had to go through a detrimental time in your life such as rape or molestation. No matter what pain you had to endure at that time in your life, I'm sure it was very painful. Birthing your purpose is as painful as that pain you had to endure during those moments. I'm sure there were times when you ask, "why me?" Or you felt like giving up and the thoughts of going through another day of living in the pain of that situation was unbearable. You may be in that moment right now. I want to encourage you, **PLEASE DO NOT GIVE UP**. You are in your birthing process; God is doing a great work in you. One thing I have learned is that there is not anything that the devil can do that God does not allow him to. God is in control of every aspect of your life. Unfortunately, we have no control over His decisions on what seem like negative situations that He allows to happen. But we can look at it for the good and say that it'll all be used for His glory. You'll be able to tell somebody how He brought you out, how He spared your life, how he turned an evil situation around and used it to help many people who are going through that same situation. Now, if you are out there living a life that is not the will of God, well you can expect to go through. But if you're in the will of God, living a life that is pleasing to Him, obeying what He has told you to do, be encouraged you're about to give birth. It will not be long before God begins to show Himself in your situation. Things are about to change and a new season is on the way. I'll share a true story with you. Years ago, there was a time when I had no car, no money, and no job; and people laughed at me and I couldn't understand why. I was so hurt and wanted God to help and to bless me, but at the time He would not. Later on I realized that, that was God's way of birthing my purpose from the pain of my past. I couldn't understand it back then, in fact, I wanted to give up and go give them all a black eye—I was just that hurt and angry. But God would not allow me to give up, nor would He allow me to do something to them that I lived to regret. I knew that God had promised me great things and I had to obey what He had told me to do at that time, and what He was going to do if I just did not give up. Have you ever been there? Ever got off focused and allowed people to rule your life by worrying about what they thought? Ever been there? One of the greatest things that you can ever do is to get delivered from people. Thank God I'm delivered. I had to stand on the word of God and He came through for me. I'm still standing, but one thing I can say is that my faith has increased to a whole new level. I'm far from perfect, I still make mistakes and wrong decisions as we all do at times, but I'm stronger and wiser now. I can say that I never would have made it without God being on my side through the most difficult times of my life. If you are going through the same thing that I went through, you can be victorious just like me. Just get back focused. I will show you how later just keep reading.

The birthing pains may be excruciating for you right now, but if you just push, push, push, push until you just can't push anymore, God will take over and push for you until your purpose comes out. You may ask, "How do I know what my purpose is?" I will answer you by saying that your purpose is what God has created you to do before you were created in your mother's womb *[Isaiah 44:2], [Jeremiah 1:5], [Jeremiah 29:11]*. Your purpose is what you were sent to the earth to do. God does not create junk. He creates you to be great and to make a difference for Him—to win souls for His Kingdom. You are not created to do what you want to do nor live the life that you want to live, you were created to live for Him and do what He wants you to do. Please do not take this wrong, but He does not want you to be a religious freak. You must keep your Christian walk in perspective. Meaning, do not be so religious to where no one understands you. Do not be so Heavenly minded, to the point where you're no earthly good. Jesus was not a religious freak. He catered to all men in order to save their souls. A perfect example, In *[Mark 2:13-17]* it talks about Jesus eating with the publicans and the sinners. The Pharisees saw this and asked the disciples why is Jesus eating with those sinners, and Jesus heard them and answered: *"They that are whole have no need of the physician, but they that are sick: I came not to call the righteous, but sinners to repentance."* Jesus came to save the world and if we say we are in Christ—belonging too, and following in the ways of Jesus Christ, we cannot be so religious that we do not see the needs of lost people. You must come down to their level in order to win them to Christ. Here is another thing that God wants you to do. He wants you to live right, treat your neighbor right, tell others that are lost and do not know Him to come to know Him; and for you to obtain a personal relationship with Him, and to love, and to give to others and not just to your familiar friends and family. This is the life that God wants you to live. You must always remember that Hell and the devil is real. Always choose to obey God's purpose when others don't. Some step out on their own and live lives that are deadly and dangerous, and lives that are not pleasing to God's word; and allow the devil to rob them from their purpose. As far as the poor, some step out on faith and some don't. It's all about trusting God to move in your finances. Expect God to move and increase your harvest as He already has promised. This is why some have died without fulfilling their purpose. And then, there are some in the prisons. Not all of them in prison are guilty, some are innocent. But if you were guilty for a crime you committed years or at times past, don't give up, it's not too late, you can still fulfill your purpose that you have been sent to this earth to do. You can still get it together and get your life back in order to do His will. You may have made mistakes, or you may be in a situation that seems as if you can never come out of it, but I'm here to tell you today that you can make a turn around, get back on the right road, and fulfill your God given purpose for your life.

If you are still alive it is not too late, you can still fulfill your purpose that you have been sent to this earth to do.

Growing up wasn't always the easy thing to do. I have had to endure some very hard trials as a young teenager. One of my greatest pains came from my dad's and my dysfunctional relationship. One day we were up, and one day we were down. It was very hard pleasing him and trying to make him proud of me. I can recall at the age of eleven I had a talent to run very fast. This talent was noticed by my middle school Physical Education coach/teacher. She called my mom and dad and told them that the school was sponsoring a special day called, "Field Day". This was a sports event where different students showed their running talents by competing in different types of sporting events. Two of the events were the fifty yard dash and the hundred yard dash. The P.E. coach/ teacher called my house and talked with my dad and he came out to see me run. Unfortunately my mom had to work on that day so she couldn't make it but was still supportive in the matter. On that day I won all of my races by a long shot. This was the start of something that seemed special between me and my dad. I was happy and excited and my dad wanted me to pursue my talent further by training out at a high school track until somebody saw me and wanted to sponsor me. Well, that day came when the high school coach of that particular High School saw my dad and me training one day and he mentioned to my dad about me running in the Junior Olympics. My dad quickly agreed and I was well on my way. He began to train me harder and harder until it became more like a job rather than a hobby. It was his first time coaching so I was his ginny pig. He was very tough, in fact, too tough. He was so tough it made me want to quit. I started hating it. We fought and argued all the time. He called me names, I called him names out of anger; and the battle went on for years. But I always respected him and wanted to obey my dad, because he was my dad and I trusted him. He was living his life through my life. I could never make him proud of me even though I won majority of all of my races that I ever ran. Later on in life I came to the realization that God allowed my life to go the way that it did because He was birthing my purpose from my pain. I cried a many a day, trying to realize why I had to go through what I was going through. Asking the question, "God why did You choose me?" I questioned why my dad treated me the way that he did. I cannot say he was all bad or tough, because he wasn't. He was still my dad and now that I'm older, wiser, stronger, and have forgiven him, I know now that he had my best interest. I can say that he loved me, even through the toughness. I can say that God has restored our relationship and we are closer now than we have ever been. My mom is happy because she always encouraged me to love and to forgive my dad—and I did. It was very hard because the thoughts of anger rose up in me every time I thought about it and I wanted to lash back at him, but God healed and I released. God has done a work in my life and in my spiritual walk. I had to literally let the past go in order for God to birth my purpose. God cannot birth your purpose when there is pain. Where there is pain, there is hurt, and where there is hurt, there is unforgiveness, and where there is unforgiveness, there is hatred. God cannot possibly do what He has planned to do in you, for you, and in your life when all of these negative things are going on. I can say that my pain came to make me stronger. It made a woman out of me. It helped me to live this thing call life. There are many other disappointments that I had to endure but I felt the need to share this testimony in order to help you who is reading this book and is holding on to the one who has hurt you, or you are holding on to your past. I have to say that the release for me is good. I want to say that the release will be good for you when you let them go. You must let the one who hurt you go in order to move on towards your future and towards your purpose. You cannot fulfill your purpose through hurt. If you think about it, how can you tell someone how to get delivered from crack cocaine when you're still using cocaine? How can you witness to someone when you're still hurt and hating your mom or dad for not loving you like she or he should have all of your life? How can you minister to a woman or man who is battling with their marriage when you're cheating on yours, or you're still hurt from when you're husband or wife cheated on you? You must be delivered and let the past go. Remember, God is ready to complete your labor pains. He's ready to take you to your new level.

Finding out what your purpose is, is simple. If you can sing, that is your purpose to sing for the Lord's purpose. If you can play an instrument, that is your purpose to play that instrument for the Lord's purpose. If you are good with counseling people, that is your purpose to counsel people for the Lord's purpose. If you can motivate, teach, counsel, or minister to a small or large group of people, that is your purpose to motivate, teach, counsel, or to minister for the Lord's purpose *[Ephesians 4:11-12, 1 Corinthians 12:3-10]*. If you are good at administrative work, that is your purpose to do administrative work for God's purpose. If you can draw, sketch, or paint, that is your purpose to draw, sketch, or paint for the Lord's purpose. There are many, many more, but these are some examples I have given to you so that you can understand how to identify what your purpose is. Got it? Hope so.

If you once were reading your bible and going to church on a regular basis but stopped because of lack of time with your schedule, or from church hurt—someone in the church who has hurt you, or you strayed away from His will because of your current life style that is not pleasing to the Lord, or because of hurt or anger from your past, repent and ask God to forgive you and allow Him to deliver you by renouncing those things that have hindered you from fulfilling His purpose that He has given you to do. Complete the short 7 Day Series of Study at the end of this chapter and purchase the Workbook to this book and make a complete turn around by living a life that is pleasing to the Lord and I know you will get that much closer to your purpose.

7 DAY SERIES OF STUDY & FAST
"BIRTHING YOUR PURPOSE FROM YOUR PAIN"

Name of Study:
Today's Date:
Focusing Scriptures:

7-DAY FAST 6AM-6PM

Eat only fruits and drink only water. You may eat soup no meats after 6pm. You will study and stand on the scriptures below by reading and confessing them daily.

MONDAY

STUDY THE CHAPTER ON THE WORD <u>PURPOSE</u>, WRITE OUT YOUR THOUGHTS ON THE SCRIPTURE FOR THE DAY AND HOW IT WILL HELP YOU AS YOU MOVE TOWARDS YOUR PURPOSE.

Ecclesiastes 3:17

TUESDAY

STUDY THE CHAPTER ON THE WORD <u>PURPOSE</u>, WRITE OUT YOUR THOUGHTS ON THE SCRIPTURE FOR THE DAY AND HOW IT WILL HELP YOU AS YOU MOVE TOWARDS YOUR PURPOSE.

Ezra 4:5

_____
_____
_____
_____

WEDNESDAY

STUDY THE CHAPTER ON THE WORD <u>PURPOSE</u>, WRITE OUT YOUR THOUGHTS ON THE SCRIPTURE FOR THE DAY AND HOW IT WILL HELP YOU AS YOU MOVE TOWARDS YOUR PURPOSE.

Ecclesiastes 3:1

_____
_____
_____
_____

THURSDAY

STUDY THE CHAPTER ON THE WORD <u>PURPOSE</u>, WRITE OUT YOUR THOUGHTS ON THE SCRIPTURE FOR THE DAY AND HOW IT WILL HELP YOU AS YOU MOVE TOWARDS YOUR PURPOSE.

Ruth 2:16

_____
_____
_____
_____

FRIDAY

STUDY THE CHAPTER ON THE WORD <u>PURPOSE</u>, WRITE OUT YOUR THOUGHTS ON THE SCRIPTURE FOR THE DAY AND HOW IT WILL HELP YOU AS YOU MOVE TOWARDS YOUR PURPOSE.

Daniel 6:17

_____
_____
_____
_____

SATURDAY

STUDY THE CHAPTER ON THE WORD <u>PURPOSE</u>, WRITE OUT YOUR THOUGHTS ON THE SCRIPTURE FOR THE DAY AND HOW IT WILL HELP YOU AS YOU MOVE TOWARDS YOUR PURPOSE.

Acts 11:23

_____
_____
_____
_____

SUNDAY

STUDY THE CHAPTER ON THE WORD <u>PURPOSE</u>, WRITE OUT YOUR THOUGHTS ON THE SCRIPTURE FOR THE DAY AND HOW IT WILL HELP YOU AS YOU MOVE TOWARDS YOUR PURPOSE.

Ephesians 1:11

_____
_____
_____
_____

LIST ALL OF THE GIFTS YOU HAVE ON THE INSIDE OF YOU. IF DO NOT KNOW THEM THEN LIST YOUR TALENTS, THOSE ARE YOUR GIFTS.

1.
2.
3.
4.
5.
6.
7.
8.
9.
10.

WRITE YOUR TESTIMONY OF HOW YOU ARE FULFILLING YOUR PURPOSE FOR THE LORD.

_____
_____
_____
_____
_____
_____

_____
_____
_____
_____
_____
_____
_____
_____

LIST ALL OF THE AREAS IN YOUR LIFE THAT YOU ARE GOING TO CHANGE IN ORDER TO FULFILL GOD'S PURPOSE IN YOUR LIFE.

1.
2.
3.
4.
5.
6.
7.
8.
9.
10.

***Purchase the Workbook for further study on this chapter*

2

Hell Faith to Heaven Faith

Hell Faith to Heaven Faith

God gave me the chapter title, "Hell Faith to Heaven Faith" as I wrote this book. I'm sure as you read this chapter, you are waiting for me to explain what hell faith to heaven faith is. Well, hell faith is when your faith is for evil verses for good, or you're an unbeliever verses a believer. Someone once told me that anything they do, they glorify themselves verses giving God all of the glory. Any accomplishments that they make, they feel that they deserve all of the glory because they are the one who accomplished it, not God. For example, say they ran a race and won. They believe that they would be the one who gave themselves the power and strength to run around the track to complete the race first. Not believing that the Lord was the one who gave them the power and the strength to run it and win. This is hell faith. True, they were the one who physically ran around the track to come in first, but what they fail to understand is the fact that they could not have done it without the help of the Lord. It was Him *[God]* who gave them all that they needed not to fall out while running around the track or falling and injuring themselves.

GOD GETS ALL OF THE GLORY

I can remember in my early teenage years when I ran track and field. There were a lot of track meets that I had to compete in during the hottest times of the day. Before my race came up, I can remember feeling as though I was going to pass out because of the excruciating heat. But right after the announcer called for the runners to step up to the line to run my particular race, I can remember getting down on the starting blocks, and as the gun blasted for all of us to take off; I shot out of the blocks and as I began to run, every thought of how hot it was out side immediately went away. Not one thought of me passing out ran through my mind. Only the thought of competitiveness of how I was going to beat my opponents to the finish line first. I can remember getting this burst of strength as I ran the race and towards the end of the race, I can remember pushing with all that I had but still having enough strength to finish. I know it was the strength of the Lord that I made it across the finish line; completing the race. I call this heaven faith. There is no way anybody can take God's glory for that. God has to get all of the glory.

If you do not believe in God, you are an unbeliever and this is what gives you hell faith. But if you believe in God and believe that He has saved you by dying for your sins; and the fact that you could not in no way have saved yourself, this is heaven faith. *[Galatians 6:14]* says, *"God forbid that we should glory in anyone or anything…"* other than the Lord, who is the only One who gives power and strength to those that are weak. No one. A Christian who believes in what the bible says about doing all to the glory of God, *[1 Corinthians 10:31]* has heaven faith. But those who do not believe this, instead they believe that they are the ones who can do everything themselves without God, is hell faith. This is what the devil believes and he tries to block the channel of faith to many of those that he can, and turn what is the truth into a lie. That's why the bible says that, *"the devil comes to steal kill and to destroy, but God comes that we might have life, and that we might have it more abundantly."* *[John 10:10]* God doesn't in no way push Himself on you, He gives you a choice. This is why He says that you <u>might</u> have life and that you <u>might</u> have it more abundantly. If you choose to have it, you will have it. If you choose not to have it, you will not have it. If you choose to have peace, you will have it. If you choose to believe that you are healed in your body, you will obtain healing, if you believe that God will turn your life around, He will do it, if you believe that God has not forgotten about you; and He will keep his promise that He has promised to you from the beginning, He will do it. But the key word is, you must believe. This is heaven faith. But if you believe that you are sick, you will be sick. If you believe that you are a failure, then you are a failure. If you believe that you are ugly and that no one cares about you or wants to date you, then you will be ugly and feel as though no one cares about you and no one will date you, this is hell faith. All of these thoughts come straight from the deceiver—the devil. He wants you to feel defeated and feel like a loser because he wants you to lose, that way you will not be focused on your purpose and eventually you will become weak and give up. But God in no way wants you to have hell faith, because this is what sends your soul to hell. But when you believe and do not doubt, and take God at His every word, this is what gets you to Heaven and allow you to have a peaceful and joyful life before getting there.

"For without faith it is impossible to please God."

In *[Hebrews 11:6] "You must believe that God is a rewarder to those who diligently seek Him."* He will in no way leave you stranded nor will God ever put you to shame in front of the enemy to laugh and to ridicule you and say all manner of evil to you and about you. God will keep His word, because He cannot lie nor can He reverse it, and that is a promise. *[Numbers 23:19-20]*

7 DAY SERIES OF STUDY
"HELL FAITH TO HEAVEN FAITH"

Name of Study:
Today's Date:
Focusing Scriptures:

7-DAY FAST 6AM-6PM

Eat only fruits and drink only water. You may eat soup no meats after 6pm. You will study and stand on the scriptures below by reading and confessing them daily.

MONDAY

STUDY THE CHAPTER ON THE WORD <u>DOUBT</u>, WRITE OUT YOUR THOUGHTS ON THE SCRIPTURE FOR THE DAY AND HOW IT WILL HELP YOU AS YOU MOVE TOWARDS YOUR PURPOSE. DOUBTING HINDERS YOUR PURPOSE.

Matthew 21:21

_____
_____
_____

TUESDAY

STUDY THE CHAPTER ON THE WORD <u>DOUBT</u>, WRITE OUT YOUR THOUGHTS ON THE SCRIPTURE FOR THE DAY AND HOW IT WILL HELP YOU AS YOU MOVE TOWARDS YOUR PURPOSE. DOUBTING HINDERS YOUR PURPOSE.

John 10:24

_____
_____
_____

WEDNESDAY

STUDY THE CHAPTER ON GOD'S <u>GLORY</u>, WRITE OUT YOUR THOUGHTS ON THE SCRIPTURE FOR THE DAY AND HOW IT WILL HELP YOU AS YOU MOVE TOWARDS YOUR PURPOSE. DOES GOD GET ALL THE GLORY IN YOUR LIFE?

1 Corinthians 10:31

_____
_____
_____

TUESDAY

STUDY THE CHAPTER ON GOD'S GLORY, WRITE OUT YOUR THOUGHTS ON THE SCRIPTURE FOR THE DAY AND HOW IT WILL HELP YOU AS YOU MOVE TOWARDS YOUR PURPOSE. DOES GOD GET ALL THE GLORY IN YOUR LIFE?

Galatians 6:14

_____
_____
_____
_____

FRIDAY

STUDY THE CHAPTER ON GOD'S PURPOSE, WRITE OUT YOUR THOUGHTS ON THE SCRIPTURE FOR THE DAY AND HOW IT WILL HELP YOU AS YOU MOVE TOWARDS YOUR PURPOSE. DOES GOD GET ALL THE GLORY IN YOUR LIFE?

Daniel 6:17

_____
_____
_____
_____

SATURDAY

STUDY THE CHAPTER ON GOD'S <u>GLORY</u>, WRITE OUT YOUR THOUGHTS ON THE SCRIPTURE FOR THE DAY AND HOW IT WILL HELP YOU AS YOU MOVE TOWARDS YOUR PURPOSE. DOES GOD GET ALL THE GLORY IN YOUR LIFE?

Revelations 4:11

SUNDAY

STUDY THE CHAPTER ON THE WORD <u>PURPOSE</u>, WRITE OUT YOUR THOUGHTS ON THE SCRIPTURE FOR THE DAY AND HOW IT WILL HELP YOU AS YOU MOVE TOWARDS YOUR PURPOSE.

Ephesians 1:11

LIST 10 AREAS WHERE YOU HAVE NOT BEEN GIVING GOD ALL OF THE GLORY.

1.
2.
3.
4.
5.
6.
7.
8.
9.
10.

WRITE YOUR TESTIMONY OF HOW YOU GAVE GOD THE GLORY AFTER SOMETHING GREAT HAPPENED IN YOUR LIFE AND YOU KNEW IT WAS ONLY HIM WHO COULD HAVE DONE IT.

_____
_____
_____
_____
_____

EXPLAIN WHAT IS, "HELL FAITH" FROM THE CHAPTER.

LIST ALL OF THE AREAS IN YOUR LIFE THAT YOU ARE GOING TO CHANGE IN ORDER TO GIVE GOD THE GLORY.

1.
2.
3.
4.

5.

6.

7.

8.

9.

10.

LIST ALL OF YOUR HELL FAITH'S THAT YOU WILL VOW TO CHANGE.

1.
2.
3.
4.
5.
6.
7.
8.
9.
10.

WRITE YOUR TESTIMONY OF THE CHANGES YOU HAVE MADE AND CAN SEE IN YOUR LIFE.

_____
_____
_____
_____
_____
_____
_____

_____
_____
_____
_____
_____
_____
_____
_____
_____
_____
_____
_____
_____
_____
_____
_____

LIST ALL OF YOUR HEAVEN FAITH'S THAT YOU WOULD LIKE TO ENHANCE.

1.
2.
3.
4.
5.

6.

7.

8.

9.

10.

***Purchase the Workbook for further study on this chapter*

3

Faith as Easy as Saying 1, 2, 3

Faith as Easy as Saying 1, 2, 3

Faith is as easy as saying 1, 2, 3. Many times we make faith seem so hard when in fact it is as easy as saying 1, 2, 3. As easy as it is to say 1, 2, 3, it is as easy to change a detrimental situation into a victorious situation. I'm reminded of Moses and the Israelites in *[Genesis chapter 14, verses 13 through 19]*. When Pharaoh's army was after them and they came to the Red Sea and there was no way around it, the Israelites panicked and attacked Moses as to why they were in the position that they were in. Moses inquired of the Lord, and the Lord told Moses to lift up the rod, and stretch it over the water and divide the water; and immediately when Moses obeyed the Lord, the waters divided and they all went across as the waters were still parted. Our faith should be just like that. As quick as the Lord told Moses to grab that rod, and stretch it over the water, and part the waters; and as quick as it did it, is as quick as the Lord will move and turn your situation around for you. Have you ever asked the Lord to move in an area and before you could get it out of your mouth good, God had already answered it, or moved in that area? Well, that's the same kind of faith I am talking about here. As quick as it takes us to say, 1, 2, 3, is as quick as it takes the Lord to answer your petition. The bible tells us that *"if we know that God hears us, by what ever we ask, we know that we have* *the petitions that we desire of him." [1 John 5:15]* So that is all the more reason to trust God in everything that you say and do. Trust God in the most challenging times of your life. I've learned that trials come to make us strong. They do not come to weaken us or make us turn a way from God and give up; they come so that we may become stronger, as we draw closer to the Father. God does not want us weak and worn out, He wants us strong and ready to fight when challenges and attacks come our way. You may be going through something that seems as though it will never change or God is never going to move, or just maybe God has told you what to do and you're too scared to do it, listen, you must obey God. He knows how much you can bear and He will never tell you to do something that He cannot back up nor will He allow shame to be brought to His name and to yours. Trust God, it will pay off. Let's take David for example in *[1 Samuel 17]*. Everybody was scared to fight the almost ten foot GIANT Philistine because they were intimidated by what they saw and by his big, weak, verbal barking words; shouting words in verse 8 like, *"...Choose a man for you, and let him come down to me!"* And, *"...I defy the armies of Israel this day; give me a man, that we may fight together!"* So the GIANT was confident in knowing that he could not be defeated. He was so confident that he challenged everybody. He appeared to have his whole armour, of course it was the armour that the world made for him and not the Lord's armour. As you read this book in the bible, remember that **<u>GIANTS DO FALL</u>**. It was proven that

Saul and the Israelites were so afraid as the bible tells us in verse 11 that they would have never gotten the nerve to stand up against the GIANT, but there was a little cute young man who was not nearly as big as the GIANT, and not nearly had the worldly type of armour that the GIANT had. But the one thing he did have was the whole armour *(his full, unwavering, assured)* spiritual armour and FAITH of the Lord *[Ephesians 6:10-18]*. Something that no one else had. He had faith in the Lord and he trusted that the Lord would give him what he needed to defeat the GIANT. It's funny because sometimes God does not give us what we expect Him too, or tells us exactly what we need to do, or where we need to go to conquer a trial, or to pass a test, or even to defeat the attacks that come our way daily. But you have to trust that what ever God gives you, **it will not fail**. I'm sure that everyone who heard and saw little David step up to fight what seemed like a huge GIANT of a man, thought that he was crazy. But sometimes you gotta' have **crazy faith**. He had crazy faith because that's how much he loved God and trusted that God would give him what ever he needed to defeat the enemy. David was a young boy and you notice I said young because young people can fight the enemy too. God will use and choose anybody He pleases. The devil doesn't care how old you are, he's going to try and fight anybody. David didn't care about being young, he was **GOD CONFIDENT**, there was no doubt in his mind that he was *not* going to be able to defeat the GIANT. Look at this, this is how confident David was in verse 38 and 39. The lack of faith was shown with Saul when he tried to give David the armour of the world, the same armour that the GIANT Goliath was wearing. David couldn't wear it because he was not used to wearing it so he took it off. This is the way you need to be when the world comes to you and tries to put their opinions on you and tell you what they think, or when they try to load you up with words that are contrary to the word of God, or try to sway you away from what God has promised you, or try to tell you what they would do. Listen to God, even if it sounds crazy or impossible to come to pass. I want to reiterate what the bible says about David not being used to wearing all of the baggage of armour that was given to him because there is a powerful revelation in it. He did not need all of the armour so he took it off. It was like he was saying: *"I don't need a bunch of baggage on, just give me Jesus! I don't need nothin' and nobody else, just give me Jesus! I've been battered and bruised, I've been talked about, people tried to scandalize my name, they said that I wasn't gon' be nothin'"*, but all David said in verse 45 was, *"…You come to me with a sword, a spear, and a javelin, but I come to you in the name of the Lord of hosts, the God of the ranks of Israel." "…all this assembly shall know that the Lord saves, not with sword and spear; for the battle is the Lord's, and He will give you into our hands."* And God did just that through David. David slung the stone, and struck the GIANT in the forehead, and he fell on his face to the earth—defeated. So it proves that **GIANTS DO FALL**, and they do not get back up. God allows giants to come into your life purposely so that God can defeat them. These words are so profound because we all have haters—people who do not like you for what ever reason, and those who lie and talk about you because either out of jealousy or just a plain ol' hateful heart. God allows them to come in your life to show you how mighty He is, and there is not one thing that they can do to harm you no matter how big of a bark they may appear to have, or how big or how tall they are in stature. Just trust God like David did because there is always promotion right behind passing a test and or an attack. You are going to be persecuted, Jesus was too. So what makes you think that you're not? But in the mist of the attacks or the trials and tribulations, God always proves Himself. And the battle is always in your favor. The battle today is in your favor! You are victorious in the Name of Jesus, amen! Do you receive that? I sure hope so.

---

*"**GIANTS DO FALL** and they do not get back up."*

You must have faith even with your family issues. Some call it family drama. I think as you read along you will agree to this, that every family has some type of dysfunctionalism. We all gotta' dysfunctional family that ain't got it all together. We all gotta' Big Mama, an Uncle Jetthrow, and a Auntie Leola Mae that just ain't gon' act right no matter how much you try to keep peace, they are going to always want to start up a fight. If you read in my first book: "When Ramona Got Her Groove Back from God", you'll find Auntie Leola Mae was the same way.

Here's a Funny Scenario:

All of the family has shown up for the family reunion or for some family occasion, and it would seem that the occasion would end peacefully. But out of nowhere a fight breaks out over who's going to take a plate home. Plates start flying and the fight begins and nobody takes anything home. This is when division comes—which is nothing but the plan of the enemy. He doesn't want families to come together, he wants them to be divided and torn a part. And this is why families go thirty years without talking to one another. Some go for a life time without talking. And just maybe a funeral would bring them back together to settle their differences, but it doesn't always go that way, they fight at the funeral.

Another Senario:

You are going to have jealous family members that will attack you especially if they see how God has favored you or they see how blessed and anointed you are, or how gifted and talented you are and they would appear not. They're going to try to tear down what God has placed inside of you. They're not going to believe the dreams and visions that God has given to you and they're not going to receive the gifts and the anointing that God has placed on your life. That brings me to Joseph and his brothers in *[Genesis 37]*. Everything seemed ok until Joseph came out and told his brothers his dream. *The first thing* that came across their minds and out of their mouths was a big laugh. It was like they said, "you ain't gon' fulfill that". They **DID NOT BELIEVE**. That is why you must be careful who you tell your vision or your dream to because they are not going to believe that God actually told or showed you that, or if it seem impossible to come to past, they are not going to believe it will. *Then second*, the bible says that they became very angry and jealous of him. They went so far as to throw him into a pit to die. You may have gone through this or you may be going through this torment right now. Your family is so jealous of you and do not believe that God can actually use you or He can't possibly give you that much money or that huge business you are believing God for, or that nice big house. And the crazy thing about it is, if you messed up and they all knew the old you, they're not going to accept the fact that God can or has forgiven you; and still has given you a huge dream that will change the nations. Even though that wasn't the case in this story because Joseph never done anything wrong for his brothers to have come against him, he was just plain ol' highly favored by God; and favored by his earthly father and his brother's did not like that. But what they failed to see was that it wasn't because Joseph was so cute, or he was so smart, or even the powerful fact that he was chosen by God, it was the purpose that God had planned for Joseph's life even before he was in his mother's womb. And that's the same case in your life. Your family is only looking at what's on the out side and the fact that you're just their sibling or you're just the lil' ol' sister or brother and there is no way that you can be the chosen one or the one who will be the most blessed or the one who will help and bless the entire family. My only encouragement for you is that you stand on the word of God, what He has told you, and stand on your vision. What ever you do, **DO NOT GIVE UP**, God is up to something in the spirit realm and in your life. The greater the test, the greater the blessing. Let me say that again, the greater the test, the greater the blessing. Here's another one. The greater the attack, the greater the anointing. Let me say that again, the greater the attack, the greater the anointing. The anointing comes with a price. But you can get through it, just don't give up, you are almost to your breakthrough. And love your family no matter how they attack you and talk bad about you. They may never believe in you or your dream, but still love them and help them in any way you can. God says in, [1 John 4:21] ..."*that he who loves God love his brother also*". So if you say that you love God, you must love your sister(s) and brother(s) and pray for them; they may not even realize that they are being used by the devil. It's not your family, it's the evil spirit of the devil that's operating inside of them.

> *"What ever you do, **DO NOT GIVE UP**,*
> *God is up to something in your life!"*

On this diagram, write in the center of the circle the ultimate area that you need to have more faith in. Where you see the lines protruding outward, write those personal areas in your life that you plan to change and write the scripture to back it up underneath. For example: write in the center, "Believing God for healing from hurt". Then on the top line write the names of the people or situations that hurt you and underneath write a scripture of healing to release them and/or the situation. From this release, you will be able to get free from them and receive the promise God has already promised you.

7 DAY SERIES OF STUDY
"FAITH AS EASY AS SAYING 1, 2, 3"

Name of Study:
Today's Date:
Focusing Scriptures:

7-DAY FAST 6AM-6PM

Eat only fruits and drink only water. You may eat soup no meats after 6pm. You will study and stand on the scriptures below by reading and confessing them daily.

MONDAY

STUDY THE CHAPTER ON THE WORD <u>FAITH</u>, WRITE OUT YOUR THOUGHTS ON THE SCRIPTURE FOR THE DAY AND HOW IT WILL HELP YOU AS YOU MOVE TOWARDS YOUR PURPOSE. DOUBTING HINDERS YOUR PURPOSE.

Romans 10:17

TUESDAY

STUDY THE CHAPTER ON THE WORD <u>VICTORY</u>, WRITE OUT YOUR THOUGHTS ON THE SCRIPTURE FOR THE DAY AND HOW IT WILL HELP YOU AS YOU MOVE TOWARDS YOUR PURPOSE. YOU ARE VICTORIOUS!

I Corinthians 15:57

_____
_____
_____
_____

WEDNESDAY

STUDY THE CHAPTER ON GOD'S <u>FAVOR</u>, WRITE OUT YOUR THOUGHTS ON THE SCRIPTURE FOR THE DAY AND HOW IT WILL HELP YOU AS YOU MOVE TOWARDS YOUR PURPOSE. GOD WILL RELEASE HIS UNMERITED FAVOUR IN YOUR LIFE.

Exodus 3:21

_____
_____
_____
_____

THURSDAY

STUDY THE CHAPTER ON GOD'S <u>FAVOR</u>, WRITE OUT YOUR THOUGHTS ON THE SCRIPTURE FOR THE DAY AND HOW IT WILL HELP YOU AS YOU MOVE TOWARDS YOUR PURPOSE.

Numbers 11:11-17

_____
_____
_____
_____

FRIDAY

STUDY THE CHAPTER ON GOD'S <u>FAITH</u>, WRITE OUT YOUR THOUGHTS ON THE SCRIPTURE FOR THE DAY AND HOW IT WILL HELP YOU AS YOU MOVE TOWARDS YOUR PURPOSE.

Habakkuk 2:4

_____
_____
_____
_____
_____
_____

SATURDAY

STUDY THE CHAPTER ON GOD'S GLORY, WRITE OUT YOUR THOUGHTS ON THE SCRIPTURE FOR THE DAY AND HOW IT WILL HELP YOU AS YOU MOVE TOWARDS YOUR PURPOSE. DOES GOD GET ALL THE GLORY IN YOUR LIFE?

Revelations 4:11

_____
_____
_____

SUNDAY

STUDY THE CHAPTER ON GOD'S GLORY, WRITE OUT YOUR THOUGHTS ON THE SCRIPTURE FOR THE DAY AND HOW IT WILL HELP YOU AS YOU MOVE TOWARDS YOUR PURPOSE. DOES GOD GET ALL THE GLORY IN YOUR LIFE?

Hebrews 2:9

_____
_____
_____

LIST ALL OF THE AREAS IN YOUR LIFE WHERE YOU HAD TO HAVE FAITH.

1.
2.
3.
4.
5.
6.
7.
8.
9.
10.

WRITE YOUR TESTIMONY OF HOW YOU HAD TO HAVE FAITH IN ORDER TO OVERCOME A CERTAIN SITUATION IN YOUR LIFE.

_____
_____
_____
_____
_____
_____

LIST ALL OF THE AREAS IN YOUR LIFE WHERE YOU HAD UNMERITED FAVOR.

1.
2.
3.
4.
5.
6.
7.
8.
9.
10.

***Purchase the Workbook for further study on this chapter**

4

Prosperity Come to Me Right Now

Prosperity Come to Me Right Now

Many Christians do not realize that we can command money to come to us instantly and it be done. God has given us the power to command blessings to come to us right away. He designed it that way, merely so that we would believe for it; and through that our faith would increase. God said that we are joint heirs with Christ *[Romans 8:17]* so this means that all of the blessings that are promised to us, is already ours but we must have the faith to believe that we can get it, and have it. The bible says in *[Matthew 21: 21] that we can say to that mountain be thou removed and be thou cast into the sea and it shall be done for you.* So what ever you believe God for, all you have to do is speak to it and it shall immediately be done for you in Heaven; and as it is done for you in Heaven, so shall it be done for you on this earth. I'm reminded about something that a preacher said in his sermon. He spoke about faith. One of the things that he spoke about was how to learn to attract the best this world has to offer. As he spoke that, my mind immediately went straight to the fact that I had been waiting on God to do everything. But what God was waiting for, was for me to get up and do it first. God has given us the power to do it ourselves through His strength, power, ability, talent, and most of all, through His faith which is through the word of God. Please do not miss your time waiting on God to make the first move. God is waiting on you to make the first move so that He can show you what He does when you show faith. God is ready to bless you and change your life forever. I have to use this scripture again because I want you to realize how powerful this scripture is. The Lord said in His Word that, *"...you shall say to this mountain be thou removed and it shall be done for you...."* And also, *"And all things, whatsoever ye shall ask in prayer, believing, ye shall receive."* *[Matthew 21:21-22]* That means to get up from your pool of slothfulness, depression, fear, lack of trust, lack of confidence, jealous of others who have already done it, and write your vision down, get your plan or your business plan together, go after that job or position that seems impossible to get, go on a fast and get in prayer; and consecration with God, and see what and where He wants you to go and do. He will never fail you, He will direct your path. *[Proverbs 3:6]* As I look back, I can remember when God spoke to me in an audible voice and told me to move to another city. It was so overwhelming that I literally thought that someone was in my home. It's funny because at the time only my dog and I lived there, and I know that my dog did not say those words. If he did I would have ran out of the house and moved that day. It did not take very long to realize that it was God. Unfortunately I did not move that same day, actually I did not move until about six to eight months later. It was the getting there and making all of the preparations to do it was what scared me. But I've learned that when God is ready to take you higher, you do not have a choice in how He does it and the way He does it. Just trust that He knows what He is doing and will not lead you astray. After those six to eight months, I can't quite remember every detailed moment but God began to deal heavily with me. He would speak to me directly and I would not obey, and He would speak to me through others while confirming what He had told me to do, and I still would not listen so He begin to bring catastrophe in my life to a point where I broke down in tears and said, "Lord I surrender, if you want me to move, then make provisions. It wasn't a week after I said that, that God did just what I had asked. Since then I cannot lie, it has not been easy everyday, and it has not been all roses either, in fact right after I first moved I questioned God, asking Him was He sure He told me to move? He assured me that He did. I was confident in what He told me to do, although at times I grew weary and angry but I still held my ground. I knew God was not punishing me, He was increasing my faith. That was a part of my promotion. He had to line my faith up with the blessings that He had promised me. If you are going through this same thing, hold your ground, God will do what He has promised. I'm a living witness that He will. There were people who doubted that God told me to move and said some damaging things, even some people and leaders in the church, but I continued to trust in God. God will fight for you just as He did for me. Do not be moved by what people say about you or to you, God will fight on your behalf. Job in the bible is a perfect example. All of the sickness and hardship that he went through was only a test. But on the outside—people looking in, it appeared that he had sinned and done something really bad, which was the reason why he went through what he went through. But in the end when his so called friends found out that it was all God who orchestrated the entire test and plan, they had to come back and repent to Job for doubting and for coming against him. You must watch your mouth at all times. You must never put your mouth on God's anointed because He will put you to an open shame. You must never judge what you think you see on the outside because you never know what God is doing. Everybody is not guilty. In *[2 Corinthians 5: 7]* it says *"...walk by faith and not by sight"*. You have to learn not to go by what you see, but go by what God has told you and showed you. Your prosperity is in your obedience. When you are obedient, you can say, "prosperity come to me right now" because you have done exactly what God has told you to do. You can make your request and watch God move and make it happen.

I can say now on this very day that God did not leave me out, He kept His promise and set me back up on my feet and blessed me with another good job, 5 published books, and a brand new blessed business called, "Heavenly Realm Publishing". He gave me the appointment, the name, the vision, and the faith to GET UP AND DO IT. Now I have accomplished publishing and printing five of my own books and have a prosperous growing company. I spoke to my money and said: "Prosperity come to me right now" and it did, and as I believe God more and increase my faith, He's going to bless me with more as He has already promised. Just as God has done this for me, He is saying to you right now that He can do the same for you. Just take Him at His word, don't allow people to get you down, speak to those mountains that are holding you back and will not move out of your way as I mentioned in the paragraph above, and command prosperity to come to you right now, and it will be done for you. Do you believe that? I sure hope so.

I believe this is the year and season for the saints to receive everything that God has promised. He said in His word that the wealth of the wicked/sinner is laid up for the just/righteous. *[Proverbs 13:22]* Everything that every crooked unbeliever, every evil person who does not regard God and lives for Him, all of their riches will be transferred to us— God's righteous. It's yours for the asking—the asking through prayer, believing by faith that you can have it. It's yours for the taking—the taking through faith believing through God's word. Asking and taking by leaning, trusting, and standing on the word of God.

---

*It's yours for the asking—the asking through prayer,
believing by faith that you can have it.
It's yours for the taking—the taking through faith
believing through God's word.*

---

7 DAY SERIES OF STUDY
"PROSPERITY COME TO ME RIGHT NOW"

Name of Study:
Today's Date:
Focusing Scriptures:

7-DAY FAST 6AM-6PM

Eat only fruits and drink only water. You may eat soup no meats after 6pm. You will study and stand on the scriptures below by reading and confessing them daily.

MONDAY

STUDY THE CHAPTER ON THE WORD <u>PROSPERITY</u>, WRITE OUT YOUR THOUGHTS ON THE SCRIPTURE FOR THE DAY AND HOW IT WILL HELP YOU AS YOU MOVE TOWARDS YOUR PURPOSE. PROSPERITY IS YOURS FOR THE ASKING.

Job 36:11

_____
_____
_____
_____
_____

TUESDAY

STUDY THE CHAPTER ON THE WORD <u>RICH</u>, WRITE OUT YOUR THOUGHTS ON THE SCRIPTURE FOR THE DAY AND HOW IT WILL HELP YOU AS YOU MOVE TOWARDS YOUR PURPOSE. GOD IS THE ONE WHO MAKES YOU RICH.

Proverbs 10:22

WEDNESDAY

STUDY THE CHAPTER ON GOD'S <u>PROSPERITY</u>, WRITE OUT YOUR THOUGHTS ON THE SCRIPTURE FOR THE DAY AND HOW IT WILL HELP YOU AS YOU MOVE TOWARDS YOUR PURPOSE. ARE YOU JEALOUS OF THOSE WHO DO EVIL TO GET WEALTH?

Psalm 73:3, Psalm 35:27

THURSDAY

STUDY THE CHAPTER ON GOD'S <u>WEALTH</u>, WRITE OUT YOUR THOUGHTS ON THE SCRIPTURE FOR THE DAY AND HOW IT WILL HELP YOU AS YOU MOVE TOWARDS YOUR PURPOSE. GOD HAS GIVEN YOU POWER TO GET GREAT WEALTH.

Deuteronomy 8:18

FRIDAY

STUDY THE CHAPTER ON GOD'S <u>NO LACK</u>, WRITE OUT YOUR THOUGHTS ON THE SCRIPTURE FOR THE DAY AND HOW IT WILL HELP YOU AS YOU MOVE TOWARDS YOUR PURPOSE. REMEMBER THERE SHALL BE NO LACK IN YOUR LIFE, MINISTRY, AND FINANCES.

2 Corinthians 8:14-15

SATURDAY

STUDY THE CHAPTER ON GOD'S <u>WEALTH</u>, WRITE OUT YOUR THOUGHTS ON THE SCRIPTURE FOR THE DAY AND HOW IT WILL HELP YOU AS YOU MOVE TOWARDS YOUR PURPOSE. KEEP THE RIGHT MOTIVES WHEN ASKING FOR WEALTH FROM GOD.

2 Chronicles 1:11-12

_____
_____
_____
_____
_____
_____

SUNDAY

STUDY THE CHAPTER ON THE WORD <u>WEALTH</u>, WRITE OUT YOUR THOUGHTS ON THE SCRIPTURE FOR THE DAY AND HOW IT WILL HELP YOU AS YOU MOVE TOWARDS YOUR PURPOSE. WEALTH AND RICHES ARE SET UP FOR GOD'S PEOPLE.

Psalms 112:3

_____
_____
_____
_____
_____

LIST ALL OF THE AREAS IN LIFE WHERE YOU NEED PROSPERITY.

1.
2.
3.
4.
5.
6.
7.
8.
9.
10.

WRITE YOUR TESTIMONY OF HOW GOD GAVE YOU WEALTH WHEN YOU LEAST EXPECTED IT.

_____
_____
_____
_____
_____
_____
_____
_____

_____
_____
_____
_____
_____
_____
_____

LIST ALL OF THE AREAS IN YOUR LIFE WHERE YOU SHARED YOUR PROPERITY AND WITH WHOM.

1.

2.

3.

4.

5.

6.

7.

8.

9.

10.

***Purchase the Workbook for further study on this chapter**

5

Don't Panic, It's Only a Test

Don't Panic, It's Only a Test

Many times in our lives we think that God is punishing us for living for Him when tests and trials come our way. But the bible tells us in *[Romans 5:1-4]* that tests, trials, and tribulations come to make us strong. They give us patience and endurance so that God's glory shall be revealed in us. I know that you have heard people say this in the church, "You see my glory, but you don't know my story." What that simply means is that, they may see the anointing that sits on you right now, but they don't know what it took for you to get it. They don't know all of the rough times you had to go through to get it, they don't know how many haters you had to endure to get it, they don't know all of the false accusers you had to make out of a liar to get it, they don't know how God came in and worked miracles and healed your body to get it, they don't know how you wanted to kill yourself because of the stress and all of the trials that were so great in your life to get it, they don't know how you were raped, molested, and abused but you overcame to get it. I thank God because He did not give up on me when I had to endure some of the hard trials in my life. I was always hated because of the multi-talents that God has given to me. I was hated because of the mighty anointing that God has placed on my life. This mainly happened in the church which I was supposed to be so respected, appreciated, and longed to find God there when I went. I had to learn that Christians are not perfect people; in fact some of them are more sinful than those that are still out there in the world. It hurt so bad when I was hurt in the church, formally called: "church hurt". This is something that I almost never got over. It hurt so bad that for a while I gave up on the church and every Pastor associated with it. I lost respect for everybody who called themselves Christians. I lost respect because we call ourselves Christians but we hurt people like it's a fad or the latest fashion statement or something. We talk to each other crazy in the mist of the service and expect sinners to come and get saved through all of that non-sense. I thought to myself, nobody else's church hurt was greater than mine. I thought that there was no way that I could overcome this. I thought that the ministry that God had given to me to do was over. But one day, something clicked inside of me, it was the voice of God telling me that it's not over and for me not to give up, it's only a test and that it's for my purpose. See God allowed them to come against me in order to push me into my destiny. All of the hell, haters, and evil workers of iniquity had to be put in place in order for God to show who He was and is today in my life. If we never have any enemies, we will never be challenged; and therefore we would get comfortable, and never go higher; therefore we would never fulfill the purpose that God has for us to fulfill. I'm reminded of a man by the name of Noah. Noah was hated against for doing the will of God. God told him to build the ark because God was tired of all the sinful things that the people were doing and because Noah was an upright and just man, God chose him to fulfill His purpose to destroy the earth. I believe God chose Noah because He knew that Noah would obey. And Noah did just that. Noah began to build the ark and of course the haters—the church folks—the people—the classmates—the neighbors—the co-workers—the so-called best friend came against what God had told Noah to do. They were too blind to see that it was the purpose of God and if they had any sense, they would have stopped being foolish and joined in with him, repented, shut their mouths, and helped him build the ark so that their lives would be saved. But they did not do that, they continued to pass judgment and talk against the will of God; and tried to discourage Noah for building and doing what God had told him to do. I love Noah because he shut out everybody and kept on fulfilling the purpose that God had chosen him to do. He did not get caught up in fights and arguments with them, he stayed focused. He knew that God would keep His promise. HE DID NOT PANIC, BECAUSE HE KNEW THAT IT WAS ONLY A TEST. It was a test when the people came against him and tried to discourage him to stop. The people were being used by the devil to try and stop the plan of God, because through this move, the covenant of Jesus Christ coming to the earth to save God's people would be fulfilled and the devil knew this and tried every avenue to stop God's plan. I'm sure the people laughed and said all kinds of evil choice words to Noah, probably threw things at him and at the ark. But he did not panic he knew that he had to pass the test. And this is the same for you, some people are assigned by the devil to come and stop the purpose of God in your life. God may have called you to be a singer for Him and there may be some singers that are already out there and are well known and they do not want you to come up because of jealousy and fear, and because they can see the anointing on your life and they know that God is going to bless you so they try and come against you and try to stop the purpose of God on your life. Or you may be just a person on your job and God has favored you by allowing your boss to give you all kinds of bonuses, raises, and promotions, and of course your co-workers—the haters, cannot stand it and they began to talk against you and go to the boss and tell lies on you that surely are not true. Or you may be someone who is in ministry and God has called you out and has favored you with the Pastor and of course the haters and the church folks—not saints of God, the church folks cannot stand it, they're calling you Mr. or Mrs. Suck-Up or the Pastor's pet. But what they failed to realize is that you were sent to the church for this season and for this hour only for the purpose of the Lord to fulfill only what God has called you to do. Or you may be someone who has multi-talents and the Lord is blessing you and of course the haters cannot stand to see you rise up and be blessed so they come against you and try to stop your purpose and get you off focused. But you stay focused and do not panic, it's only a test because if God made you a promise, He does not stagger, meaning He does not do it through unbelief, but is fully persuaded that what ever He promised you, He is more than able to perform it. Here is scripture to back it up. *[Romans 4:20-21]*, God says, *"...that He staggers not at the promise through unbelief; but was strong in faith, giving glory to God." [21] And "...being fully persuaded that, what He had promised, He was more than able also to perform."*

Being sick in our bodies is not fun; in fact it seems that once the doctor has diagnosed you with the sickness, it would seem that the right thing to do would be to get ready for your burial, but I want you to know that God gets the last word. He gets the final say. It goes back to the fact that God does not stagger at His promise. What ever you are going through, and no matter what sickness you have been diagnosed with; and no matter how detrimental the sickness is, God still does not stagger at His promise, He is more than able to perform it— HE WILL PERFORM IT! I am a living witness. There was a large lump in my throat that was once the size of almost a golf ball. When I went to get it checked out, the doctor said that it was a Goiter and practically harmless. I do not care if it was only harmless; I knew that it was not supposed to be there. It was very painful at times it caused great discomfort when I swallowed. It bothered me so bad that I had to go to the hospital's emergency room for help. I went to the emergency room and stayed there for over three hours until I finally saw the doctor. When the doctor checked me out, all he said was again, it's just a Goiter and it's practically harmless. I went home and began to pray. Later as I read the word of God, I read about how Jesus laid hands on the sick and the bible says that they recovered and were healed. The Holy Spirit quickened my spirit and said that "Jesus has left you that same power". I began to fast, pray, believe, and to take God at His word on what the bible says about being healed from all manner of sickness. In *[Isaiah 53:5]* it prophetically says that, *"...he was wounded for our transgressions, he was bruised for our iniquities; the chastisement of our peace was upon him; and with his stripes we are healed."* When I stood on this scripture and began to believe God, the Goiter went down from the size of almost a golf ball to the size of a dime within seconds. I was not satisfied with that because that was not what God promised me. He promised me that He would heal me completely — remember in His word He said: *"...by his stripes you are healed."*? Well, that means **COMPLETELY HEALED**. I began to believe God for complete healing. Well honestly to say I did not begin believing God for my complete healing right away. I was upset with God and thought that He was a respect of persons or just had not planned to heal me completely. I was mistaken. It is God's ultimate plan that we, His people, prosper and be in good health even as our souls prosper *[3 John 2]* God wants us well in order to do His will and to fulfill His purpose. All He wants us to do is to release our faith and trust Him to move. I did a short study on Abraham, and saw how close Abraham and the Lord was. Abraham was God's friend and there was nothing that God could keep from him, and even to that matter, wanted to keep anything from him. *[Genesis 18:17] Amplified* Abraham had that much faith and favor with the Lord. God knew that He could trust him to do what ever he was supposed to do, which was to fulfill the purpose and covenant that God had made with him to become a great nation. My point in using Abraham, which is a great example, was to say that God has made you and me a covenant. We have to petition the covenant that He has made with us. The same covenant God made with Abraham is the same covenant that God has made with us because we are descendants of Abraham. God made a covenant with me in his word that I am healed, and I proclaimed that. The Goiter has been removed from my body through God's healing. Praise God! God kept is word and His covenant just like He did for Abraham. The covenant that God has made with you, whether He spoke it audibly to you, in your heart, or He spoke it through His word, I am standing with you that it will manifest on this year! This is your year! Remember, tests only bring testimonies. Do not use the stumbling blocks that came in your life as something that came to bring shame and a way to stop you, but look at them as tests that came to bring testimonies. God will never allow stumbling blocks to conquer you. Amen? Amen. Do you agree? Sure hope so!

Trials come to make you strong. God uses trials and tests as a time to try your faith. He uses them to see if you are going to listen, obey, and totally depend on Him; especially when the enemy is right before you. The enemy can attempt to work in different areas of your life. He doesn't just come in the form of sickness, but he comes to attack your finances, your peace, your love, your joy, your mind, your thoughts, in your relationships, in your family, and on your job. All of God's people go through tests and trials. But when you encounter this in your life, it's not a time to roll over and die, it's a time to get up, do not be moved, and a time to stay in a peaceful position. *[Psalms 55:22]* The bible clearly states that the righteous should not be moved when trouble or trying times come our way. It's a time to pick up the word of God, go in prayer, and see how God wants you to get through your particular tests with the victory. And you will notice that as you listen, obey, and totally depend on God, you will be stronger and wiser when or if that test tries to come again in your life. Understand? I sure hope so.

Tests are not always the easiest thing[s] to past especially when the situation you're in is not your fault, or the attack that has come against you is really crazy and is obvious that it's the devil's attacks and is a trial that you must pass. But I can guarantee you that God will never put more on you than what you can bear. He will always make a way of escape and give you a victorious end. *[I Corinthians 10:13]*

There may have been a time in your life when something happened to you that was not your fault and you could not understand why you had to endure that. For example, you may have gone to the doctor to get tests ran for a minor routine check up, and came away with results that you have the AIDS [HIV] virus. They told you that you transmitted it through a dirty needle a doctor used or you got it from your partner that told you they would never cheat on you. Just hearing that can be very detrimental to a point that suicide is your only option, or going to them and murdering them. I'm here to tell you, you do not have to turn to suicide, murder, or to a state of depression; to a point where you will not talk, eat, or sleep. You still have a victorious end! It is not the end of the world for you! You can overcome this! Don't make the devil happy to take your life, or someone else's life, or to put you in that position of mute and torment. God can and will heal you from anything. There is nothing too hard for God! *[Jeremiah 17:32]* The devil came to destroy you, but God will use it for His glory. You will tell thousands of what God has done for you. You will not die, but you will live and declare God's glory. *[Psalms 118:17]*

TEST'S ONLY BRINGS **TEST**IMONIES

7 DAY SERIES OF STUDY
"DON'T PANIC, IT'S ONLY A TEST"

Name of Study:
Today's Date:
Focusing Scriptures:

7-DAY FAST 6AM-6PM

Eat only fruits and drink only water. You may eat soup no meats after 6pm. You will study and stand on the scriptures below by reading and confessing them daily.

MONDAY

STUDY THE CHAPTER ON THE WORD <u>TESTIMONIES</u>, WRITE OUT YOUR THOUGHTS ON THE SCRIPTURE FOR THE DAY AND HOW IT WILL HELP YOU AS YOU MOVE TOWARDS YOUR PURPOSE.

Psalms 119:95

TUESDAY

STUDY THE CHAPTER ON THE WORD <u>TRIAL</u>, WRITE OUT YOUR THOUGHTS ON THE SCRIPTURE FOR THE DAY AND HOW IT WILL HELP YOU AS YOU MOVE TOWARDS YOUR PURPOSE. TRIALS COME TO MAKE YOU STRONG. THEY ARE THE TRYING OF YOUR FAITH.

I Peter 4:12-16

WEDNESDAY

STUDY THE CHAPTER ON THE WORD <u>PERSECUTION</u>, WRITE OUT YOUR THOUGHTS ON THE SCRIPTURE FOR THE DAY AND HOW IT WILL HELP YOU AS YOU MOVE TOWARDS YOUR PURPOSE.

Romans 8:35

THURSDAY

STUDY THE CHAPTER ON THE WORD <u>TESTIMONY</u>, WRITE OUT YOUR THOUGHTS ON THE SCRIPTURE FOR THE DAY AND HOW IT WILL HELP YOU AS YOU MOVE TOWARDS YOUR PURPOSE. YOU OVERCOME THE ENEMY BY YOUR TESTIMONY.

Revelation 12:11

FRIDAY

STUDY THE CHAPTER ON THE WORD <u>WARFARE</u>, WRITE OUT YOUR THOUGHTS ON THE SCRIPTURE FOR THE DAY AND HOW IT WILL HELP YOU AS YOU MOVE TOWARDS YOUR PURPOSE. GOD PULLS DOWN EVERY STRONGHOLD.

2 Corinthians 10:4

SATURDAY

STUDY THE CHAPTER ON THE WORD <u>FEAR</u>, WRITE OUT YOUR THOUGHTS ON THE SCRIPTURE FOR THE DAY AND HOW IT WILL HELP YOU AS YOU MOVE TOWARDS YOUR PURPOSE. DO NOT FEAR, GOD WILL GIVE YOU A SOUND MIND IN THE MIST OF YOUR TRIAL.

2 Timothy 1:17

_____
_____
_____
_____
_____
_____

SUNDAY

STUDY THE CHAPTER ON THE WORD <u>LOVE</u>, WRITE OUT YOUR THOUGHTS ON THE SCRIPTURE FOR THE DAY AND HOW IT WILL HELP YOU AS YOU MOVE TOWARDS YOUR PURPOSE. LOVE YOUR ENEMIES.

Matthew 5:44

_____
_____
_____
_____
_____
_____

LIST ALL OF THE AREAS IN LIFE WHERE YOU ENCOUNTERED MAJOR TEST AND TRIALS THAT YOU PASSED.

1.

2.

3.

4.

5.

6.

7.

8.

9.

10.

WRITE YOUR TESTIMONY OF HOW YOU OVERCAME A DETRIMENTAL TEST IN YOUR LIFE THAT ALMOST TOOK YOUR LIFE.

_____
_____
_____
_____
_____
_____
_____

_____
_____
_____
_____
_____
_____
_____

LIST ALL OF THE AREAS IN YOUR LIFE THAT ARE TESTS THAT YOU WILL MAKE A VOW TO PASS.

1.

2.

3.

4.

5.

6.

7.

8.

9.

10.

***Purchase the Workbook for further study on this chapter*

6

It's a Set Up

It's a Set Up

It's a set up that you are in the position that you are in right now. Every part of your life whether great or small, bad or good, rich or poor, lacking or no lack, struggling or free, is a set up by the Lord. God knew that you would be in the position that you are in right now. Yes right now! I know you are asking, "How can it be possible that God would allow me to go through this struggle alone or how could it be possible that God would pile all of these bills up to a point where I can't pay for them? And how could it be possible that God would allow my children to disobey and come against me? How could it be possible that God would allow the state to take my children? How could it be that God would allow my mom and dad to disown me? How could it be possible that God would allow the devil to make my momma get hooked on crack cocaine and my daddy be put in prison?" Well, I'm here to tell you that God will not put more on you than what you can bear. At times in your life, trials and situations come, and you feel as if God don't do something, you are not going to make it. You feel like you're going to loose your mind. You hear some bad news, the friend you trusted all of your life has just betrayed you, you just lost your job and bills are piled up to a point that you and your family are about to be put out on the street. You are about to foreclose on the home that God said that He would pay off. You just got word that your child just got put in jail for murder or for drugs. You are going through a terrible battle with divorce and trying to get custody of your children. The man or woman that you thought you were going to spend the rest of your life with has just jumped on you and abused you in such a way that you do not know whether you are going to live. You had a bad accident and the doctor told you that you will live, but you will loose both of your legs. You may be young and you feel as if your parents or your so called friends don't love or understand you. They disowned you. You don't feel any use of going any further. These situations seem detrimental. But I want you to be encouraged. God says in *[Romans 8:18] "...that we reckon that the sufferings of this present time are not worthy to be compared with the glory which shall be revealed in us."* The suffering that you are going through can not be compared to the glory and the testimony that God will use through you to show the world His glory. God will reveal in and through you to show how you overcame, how you did not give up, how you did not give in, and how you got the victory to carry on and still make it to the top. God is using your life as a testimony for His glory. Don't you know that just as bad as your situation is right now, there is someone else in this world that is going through something worse than you? The bible says in *[Ecclesiastes 3:1-15] "...that there is a season, and a time to every purpose..."* [4] *"...A time to cry and time to laugh..."* [8] *"...a time of war, and a time of peace."* Honestly to say that it's a set up. This is the time for you to trust God with all that you have. Giving up cannot be in your vocabulary. You cannot give up, God is with you---it may not seem like it, but trust Him, He is. He's watching what's going on in your life. There is not one thing that you can tell God that He does not already know. He knows how you feel, he knows what you do not have, He knows how hurt you are, He knows how upset you are, He knows that you feel as if you're one step away from suicide---not an option, and He knows how your enemies are coming against you. He never said fulfilling your purpose was going to be easy at times. Ask Jesus, He will tell you how challenging it was to fulfill the purpose and will of God while He was here on the earth, but the good news is, is that He did not give up, he said in *[Matthew 26:36-42]* to the Father as he prayed in Gethsemane: *"...nevertheless not as I will, but as thou wilt."* Jesus was going through—He was troubled, and afraid; and He knew his time was near to go through much suffering for our sins. So that right there alone should encourage you that if Jesus survived through an unbearable beating and crucifixion, you can survive through what ever you are going through, just for a season. Amen? Amen. Praise God! That's good news that you can know that you are victorious and that God will never leave you nor will He forsake you. *[Numbers 23: 19-20]* He knows and He is on the way, for the battle is not yours it's the Lord's. *[2 Chronicles 20: 15-18]* You should worship the Lord right where you are because the battle that you are in right now is not yours it's the Lords, and I have never known a battle that God did not win. It's a set up! God is still in control! God is still on the Throne! He's right there ready to take the burden from you so that you can live and have new life—life of peace, joy, love, and liberty! Hallelujah! Praise God! God's people win, we do not loose!

As I write this book God is reminding me of Abraham and Sarah. In *[Genesis 15]* God made a covenant with Abraham that if he could count the number of stars in the sky that would be the number of descendents that he would have. And he inquired of God that how he could give him this promise concerning all of Abraham's descendents seeing that he had no children. And God told him that if he could count the number of stars, so will his descendents be. Then God comes back in chapter 17 and makes another covenant with Abraham. First, He changes Abraham's name from Abram to Abraham. Second, God tells him that he shall be the father of many nations. Third, the covenant God makes with Abraham was about circumcision and Abraham's seed. Then last, here is the highlight of the revelation that God is making here: if you will look in verses 15-21, God is still speaking to Abraham as Abraham is still on his face. God is telling Abraham here that Sarah shall be the mother of many nations and that she shall bear a child—which was a boy. If you look back in chapter 15, verses 2-3, where Abraham is petitioning God concerning what God told him that he would do. God promised him that he would have a child from his own bowels/body, found in verse 4. This is my point to all of this, God promised Abraham that he would give him a child even before Abraham could see what God was doing. That's why Abraham questioned in verses 2-3 that how could he be blessed with descendants when he did not have any children, and God quickly assured him that if he could count the stars in the sky, so shall his descendants be. Now if you move to chapter 17, God comes back and completes his promise—His covenant that he made with Abraham back in chapter 15. He tells Abraham that Sarah that they will have a son even though she was as old as she was and also the fact that she could not have any children. You can clearly see that God was ready to keep His promise that He made with Abraham, and it's obvious that Abraham and Sarah must have gotten a breakthrough in prayer. If you are in question as to whether or not Sarah could have any children read in chapter 16. The bible clearly says that in verse 2 that she could not. This shows without any question that God specializes in keeping His promise. It's funny as I read that God did not do it right a way because He wanted to increase their faith. In chapter 15 God makes the promise of the descendants, in chapter 16, verse 2, God shows here that Sarah could not have any children, and in chapter 17, the promise is fulfilled in verses 15-21 that God will establish his covenant/promise that he will bear them a son and God even gave them the name of the child—called him Isaac. And last, in chapter 21:1-2, God did fulfill his promise—he gave Sarah, Isaac her son. Now here is where the enemy came in as we go back. God made a covenant with Abraham concerning that Sarah will have a child and if you read in chapter 16, it says that Sarah knew that she could not have a child so, here is the mistake she made, she told Abraham since she could not have a child he could sleep with Hagar and have a child. She made her his secondary wife. I believe that this was not a part of the promise, it was for Sarah to have the child that God had promised, but Sarah looked at the outer appearance—what she could see in the natural and not what God had promised in the spiritual, and encouraged her husband to sleep with another women (Hagar). This is how the enemy came in. Because Sarah made this wrong choice, in verses 4-6, this caused strife with them and they had a fight all because Sarah did not wait on the Lord to keep His promise, which came in chapter 17, that God made with Abraham that Sarah would have a son and the covenant would be fulfilled. In reading this lengthy example through God's word, you must always remember that God will never just talk, make a statement, or say a bunch of lies and know that He's not going to do what He say He will do. He will always come through. Many times God has made us these same types of promises that do not happen right away, so we get anxious or we get tired or frustrated, and we go ahead of God and make crazy mistakes that would not have been made if we only waited on the Lord. Even though some good still came out of Hagar having Ishmael (Abraham's other son), which blessings were on his life as well, but that still was not the initial promise that God had made with Abraham. As I said before, this is why you must wait on God and do not go ahead of Him, and make choices that you think will be the best choice, when really it is the trick of the enemy. God's covenant never changes, **IF HE MADE YOU A PROMISE, IT MUST COME TO PAST.**

God does not stagger at His promise, He does not change His mind, He does not doubt or fall into unbelief, or even have temper tantrums, He's more than able to perform His word; and He takes joy in it. He is fully persuaded that what He had promised, He is MORE THAN able to perform it. [Romans 4: 20-21]

I thought I was finished with this chapter but God has given me another revelation so I better write it down. I like to use all sorts of adhesives at times when making crafty 3-D objects in my spare time and 3-D models and blue prints during my years of teaching on the high school and on the college level. One of those adhesives I use is called: "Elmer's Glue-All". It is a Multi-PURPOSE GLUE. The story is, I was working on an assignment at the time and the assignment called for the need to use the Elmer's Glue-All. As I worked on the computer and gathered some saved drawings, my eyes happened to glance over to the glue as my eye balls quickly fixed on the words, "PURPOSE GLUE, BONDS STRONG FOR ALL YOUR NEEDS." Most people use this glue all the time and never pay any attention to those powerful words. They quickly spoke out to me as I began reading them over and over and over again. The word: **"PURPOSE"** was the first to ring out, then, **"GLUE…BONDS STRONG FOR ALL YOUR NEEDS"** rang out next. The word: **"purpose"** signified that the glue had a certain purpose and that purpose was strictly intended for the use of making something stick and hold together. And then the words: **"Glue….Bonds strong for all your needs"**, signified to me that the glue was strong and would fulfill all of your needs no matter what you use it for. It didn't say some of your needs; it said all of your needs. The revelation in this, as far as what God has shown me, was that God is the supplier of all of your needs according to His word in *[Philippians 4:19]*. Just as this type of glue is intended for the use of adhesively bonding something together, this is what God is to your life—He sticks to you like glue in order for you to come into the knowledge of who He is; and He pushes you to accomplish what purpose He has called, anointed, and appointed you to accomplish. After you, by faith confess, accept, believe, and receive Him into your heart, mind, spirit, and soul, He promises you that He will supply all of your needs according to His riches and glory by Christ Jesus. God is strictly intended to supply everything you stand in need of according to the purpose in which He has already set for you to accomplish. For example, if God has called, chosen, and purposed for you to be a teacher, He will supply everything you need in order to first become a teacher, then to be able to teach efficiently, effectively, and to supply all you need in order to fulfill the purpose as to why He called you to teach in that particular field, and in that particular school in the first place. This was an awesome revelation that God gave to me. I could not pass up giving it to you. You may be believing God to save your family; not realizing that He has called you to do it. I'm here to tell you don't panic, God promises that He will supply all that you will need in order to fulfill the great task that lies ahead of you. The same goes with any other area that He has called you to complete.

Just as this type of glue is intended for the use of adhesively bonding something together, this is what God is to your life—He sticks to you like glue in order for you to come into the knowledge of who He is; and He pushes you to accomplish what purpose He has called, anointed, and appointed you to accomplish.

All you have to do is remember to stay focused on God's word, pray, and seek His face. Go on a fast regularly, and always know that He is here to supply all of your needs. So no matter what you are going through, just know it's only a set-up. God does not come to make you loose or to destroy you, He comes to bless you and to give you an expected end. [Jeremiah 29:11]

7 DAY SERIES OF STUDY
"IT'S A SET UP"

Name of Study:
Today's Date:
Focusing Scriptures:

7-DAY FAST 6AM-6PM

Eat only fruits and drink only water. You may eat soup no meats after 6pm. You will study and stand on the scriptures below by reading and confessing them daily.

MONDAY

STUDY THE CHAPTER ON THE WORD <u>POSITION</u>, WRITE OUT YOUR THOUGHTS ON THE SCRIPTURE FOR THE DAY AND HOW IT WILL HELP YOU AS YOU MOVE TOWARDS YOUR PURPOSE. THE SCRIPTURE DOES NOT SPECIFICALLY SAY THE WORD, "POSITION", BUT THERE IS A REVELATION.

Genesis 39:20-21

TUESDAY

STUDY THE CHAPTER ON THE WORD <u>PLACE</u>, WRITE OUT YOUR THOUGHTS ON THE SCRIPTURE FOR THE DAY AND HOW IT WILL HELP YOU AS YOU MOVE TOWARDS YOUR PURPOSE. ARE YOU IN THE RIGHT PLACE?

Psalms 118:5

WEDNESDAY

STUDY THE CHAPTER ON THE WORD <u>STRENTGH</u>, WRITE OUT YOUR THOUGHTS ON THE SCRIPTURE FOR THE DAY AND HOW IT WILL HELP YOU AS YOU MOVE TOWARDS YOUR PURPOSE. GOD IS YOUR STRENGTH.

Psalms 28:8

THURSDAY

STUDY THE CHAPTER ON THE WORD <u>POWER</u>, WRITE OUT YOUR THOUGHTS ON THE SCRIPTURE FOR THE DAY AND HOW IT WILL HELP YOU AS YOU MOVE TOWARDS YOUR PURPOSE. GOD HAS GIVEN YOU POWER.

2 Samuel 22:33

_____
_____
_____
_____
_____

FRIDAY

STUDY THE CHAPTER ON THE WORD <u>FOCUS</u>, WRITE OUT YOUR THOUGHTS ON THE SCRIPTURE FOR THE DAY AND HOW IT WILL HELP YOU AS YOU MOVE TOWARDS YOUR PURPOSE.

Psalms 91

_____
_____
_____
_____
_____
_____

SATURDAY

STUDY THE CHAPTER ON THE WORD TIME, WRITE OUT YOUR THOUGHTS ON THE SCRIPTURE FOR THE DAY AND HOW IT WILL HELP YOU AS YOU MOVE TOWARDS YOUR PURPOSE. TIME IS AN ESSENCE.

Genesis 4:3

SUNDAY

STUDY THE CHAPTER ON THE WORD BLESSINGS, WRITE OUT YOUR THOUGHTS ON THE SCRIPTURE FOR THE DAY AND HOW IT WILL HELP YOU AS YOU MOVE TOWARDS YOUR PURPOSE. BLESSINGS COME FROM GOD.

Proverbs 19:12, Ephesians 1:3

LIST ALL OF THE AREAS IN YOUR LIFE WHERE YOU ARE NOT FOCUSED.

1.
2.
3.
4.
5.
6.
7.
8.
9.
10.

WRITE YOUR COMMITMENT ON HOW YOU PLAN TO GET BACK FOCUSED AFTER READING THE SCRIPTURES ABOVE ON THIS WEEK.

_____
_____
_____
_____
_____
_____

_____
_____
_____
_____
_____
_____
_____
_____

LIST ALL OF THE AREAS IN YOUR LIFE THAT YOU PLAN TO CHANGE IN ORDER TO STAY FOCUSED.

1.
2.
3.
4.
5.
6.
7.
8.
9.
10.

***Purchase the Workbook for further study on this chapter*

7

Iron Sharpens Iron

Faith Session 2

Iron Sharpens Iron

Do you have a friend or are you in a relationship where you love that or those persons dearly but you two/all fight all the time? Do you ever allow the devil to play with your emotions and make you feel as if no one loves you? You may be there right now. Do you ever feel as if you just don't want to be bothered, and your friend, or husband, or wife, or family member, want to come and pour all of their bad day and problems out on you? Are you a selfish person who wants your way all the time? Is it hard for you to say you're sorry or admit when you're wrong? Do you seek to control people? Are you jealous of others accomplishments and feel left out? Do you live a lifestyle that contradicts the word of God? These are the areas that God wants to sharpen and clean out. God comes to sharpen these areas that seem impossible to sharpen. Think of how hard iron is but yet it can be sharpened. The only one that can sharpen it is a carpenter—someone who has the tools and is equipped to do it. In this case, Jesus, who is the carpenter is the One who is in control of sharpening these very areas in your life that are struggles, which are sent from the devil to stop your progress in who God wants you to be and how He wants you to act. This is what is meant by iron sharpens iron. God always wants to clean His people up because He wants us to walk and operate in the image of Him. He doesn't want you going around hurting others feelings by having a bad attitude. He doesn't want you to think about yourself and always want to be right. Nobody is right all the time and you can't have your way all the time, you must share and love. This is what God teaches us in His word. You have to be patient with others when they are going through and want to talk to you, even when it's at a time when you just don't feel like being bothered. What will help you to be patient is to think about a time when you needed a listening ear and someone was there to listen to you. God knows when people are trying to use you for a trash can rather than a listening, ministering ear and He will not allow them to pull on you and bring you down and make you heavy. Then you feel worse than they did before they ever came to you in the first place.

God is always convicting us in areas that we need to change. Kind of like the refiners fire and the fullers soap. *[Malachi 3:2-3]* God is a refiner and a purifier. He comes to purify everything that needs to be made clean. This is also like the potters wheel—the potter and the clay. *[Jeremiah 18: 1-6]* Have you ever been in the fire or on God's Potter's Wheel? God is the Potter, and you be the clay. Trust me, it does not feel good. When I first accepted God as my Lord and Savior I thought all of my troubles, hurts, and pains were going to go away, when actually they had just begun. Let me make you understand what I mean by this phrase before you think

Position Your Faith for Great Success

about judging the matter. Before I was saved, I had troubles, pains, hurts, and a bunch of heartaches that I could not handle. I was literally defeated and had no where to turn too because I did not have the Lord on my side and in my life. But the minute I turned to the Lord, all of my troubles, pains, hurts, and heartaches did not stop—but went to another level. The level that I'm speaking of was a level of trusting God to change *my mind*—my way of thinking on how I saw things. *My emotions*—how I thought no one loved me and couldn't trust people because of past hurts and disappointments. M*y attitude*—how I reacted and perceived things, moving without consulting God first. *My actions*—how I treated others and my own way of doing things. So when I say that they did not stop, well that was true, they did not. But instead of going through them defeated without the Lord, I overcame them with trusting in Him with His strength, and not my own after I accepted Him into my heart, mind, spirit, soul, and life. He gave me a new mind—a renewed mind. *[Ephesians 4:23]* I had a new way of approaching my troubles. I had a *new attitude*, a new way of thinking about the people I could not get along with. *My actions* were that I accepted the fact that I was going to have enemies that did not like me for what ever reason. I had to realize that people were going to reject me because of who I represented. People did not want to be around me and thought I was a holy-rolly because I talked, walked, and lived Jesus. The greater the anointing, the greater the expectations. When you have a great anointing on your life, you are going to be a target for rejection because most people cannot relate to you. They can't find the familiar—what they can identify with. So they judge. They fear. They talk bad about you. They mimic your actions and how you talk. They watch your every move. They try to find something bad about you and expose it to the world. But even in their evil ways, God still delivers and He lifts up a standard against them. *[Isaiah 59:19]* Then most of all, I realized more that God was my ultimate superior. He was and still is my first choice of how I react to things, and how I think about things, and life right now. I must admit that this did not happen over night, it took some going through the refiner's fire and a whole lot of sittin' on the Potter's Wheel, as I mentioned earlier. It took trial and error, it took some fallin' on my face and having to get up with some scares that didn't heal very easy. This may be happening in your life. You may be going through the same things that I have gone through; if so, God is delivering and cleansing you. Sometime people think that it's because of you as to why you need to be delivered, but it's not always you, sometimes it's from others who have scarred you, have come against you, and have attacked you. You must release them. This can cause you to sit on the refiner's wheel so that He can cleanse you and set you free from it all, and them all. God is working on your mind, attitude, and actions.

He's changing the way you think, the way you react, and the way you act towards others. My mother always told me, "you treat others like you want to be treated. And you love people and do not hate those who mistreat you. Ask God to bless them and help them with their evil ways." This is how we all should be. Never try to do evil for evil. And certainly, do not do evil yourself. You cannot make innocent people pay because you're unhappy about your past, hurts, disappointments, and the way your current situation is going. You should turn to the Lord for help and He will help you by delivering you. Do not allow the enemy to bring pride in your heart and life by thinking that you do not have any problems and you can handle the situation yourself. Let go and let God deliver you. I guarantee you, you will not regret it.

I can recall a scripture that we should all be very familiar with, [Romans 12:2]. We can do surgery on this scripture as it first says in verse 2: *"Be not conformed to this world:...."* Now what does this mean? This simply means for you who belong to God, that you do not fashion your ways, attitudes, and actions after this world. The bible says in, [John 17:16, and in, 1 John 2:15-17] *"...we are in the world, but we are not of the world."* This means that we do not act like people who do evil things—things that are against the word and will of God. The next part of this scripture says, *"but be ye transformed by the renewing of your mind..."* Now here is the key part of this entire scripture. It is the highlight of what I have been talking about during this entire chapter. In order to know that you have the victory over all of your troubles and problems, you have to know that they do not belong to you anymore; they belong to the Lord. You are going to go through persecutions, and you are going to suffer at one point in your life, but God promises us that in *[1 Peter 3:14] "...that to suffer for righteousness' sake, happy are you..."* What this means is that while you are going through your suffering for that season—meaning it won't last always. God says that you will be happy. He will make sure that you are well taken care of and the enemy is defeated. You will have all the joy you need, you will have all the peace you need, and then you will have all of the love you need to get through that particular test. My mother always told my siblings and I when we were growing up that, "we may not have what we want, but we should always thank God that we got what we need." We did not have a lot of money therefore we did not have very many clothes to wear, nor did we have a lot of food to eat at times. There were many days where we had to wear the same things over and over again and eat seconds, thirds, and wonder where the fourths were going to come from. If you look at this story, I just said that we did not have the clothes we wanted nor the best choice food, but we had clothes that we needed in order to clothe our bodies and food to keep us from starving. When I was young I did not understand why we had to go through this and live like this, but my mother always assured my brother's and I that things would get better. I got mad at her words because my young immature mind was looking at the current situation and was not mature enough to know what God said to my mother about our future and certainly about mine. God has promised us blessings if we keep His commandments. *[Deuteronomy 28:1-14]* Now that I have a mature, renewed mind and a whole new way of looking at things and life, I can now go through suffering and persecutions differently because I'm not looking at the current—the situation that I'm in right at this moment, I'm looking at my future—what God has promised me. I'm looking at my purpose. I'm waiting on God to fulfill His promises, which are the blessings that He has promise to give. This is what you have to do. You cannot look at your current situation. You have to look a head towards your future—at what God has promised you. God never makes a promise that He does not keep. He will always keep His word. Now where you go wrong is when you go off on your own and do your own thing. You are not operating in your renewed mind you are operating like the world operates, not with love and by what is right, but with hatred, backstabbing, jealousy, pride, and with brutal actions.

The last part of this scripture says: *"...that ye may prove what is that good, and acceptable, and perfect will of God."* This basically says that you may ***"prove"*** yourself—basically who you are in Christ. You are the King's Kid. You belong to the Almighty God, there is non like Him, this is how you prove who you are and who you belong to. And then what is ***"acceptable"*** in God's site. You want to make sure that you do everything that is acceptable in God's site. Some may say: "Why do I have to do everything right in God's site, it ain't like He can see me?"

Well sorry to burst your bubble but God see and know everything. There is nothing that can get past God nor is there anything that He does not already know. In fact, He knows before you know. He's omnipresent. While He's with you, He's with me. While He's watching you, He's watching me. *[Deuteronomy 20:4]* And He knows what you are going through and doing at all times. I have to laugh at this because some of us think that we can hide and sneak from God. But we can't, He even knows what we are thinking. He knows our thoughts better than we know our own thoughts. His thoughts are not our thoughts; and His ways are not our ways. *[Isaiah 55:8]* And then last, the **"perfect will of God"**. Most people are satisfied with only the permissive will of God. This is the will where God permits you to receive what ever <u>YOU</u> want, where as the perfect and divine will of God is where you are in the will that <u>HE</u> has predestined for you to be in. This will is the exact will that you want to be in because it is the highest will you can be in. When you think of something perfect and divine, there is not anything that can be better or perfect than this will. God tells us in His word to "...*be perfect just as He is perfect*". *[Matthew 5:48]* That's a tough pill to swallow, because I have to admit, it is very hard being perfect like our Father in Heaven is. I mean He's perfect and no one can top Him; and no one can be better than He is. I'm sure that is why He says, *be perfect as He is*. I can recall one day that I tried to be perfect all day. And just as I was trying to be perfect, here came the tests. I was tested on every hand to see if I would stay perfect in each test that came my way during that day. One of those test were the test to love when the enemy was in my face cursing and yelling all kinds of words other than calling me a child of God. I was tempted to yell and curse back at them. Trying to be perfect was truly the last thing on my mind—and certainly I wasn't trying to quote scriptures and speak in other spiritual tongues either. But I had to remember that I was trying to be perfect and that I was being tested. Fortunately I passed the test because I did not curse and yell back at them. I stayed quiet and then when I had a chance to speak, they were all worn out from yelling. But on the other hand I can recall on another occasion when I wasn't so perfectly strong. I had an encounter with a person that was allowing the devil to use him by first picking at me to try and get me started so that I could argue back with him. I tried to avoid and dodge the punches through his words, but it wasn't working. The more I stayed quiet, the more frustrated he became and was claiming that I was ignoring him and started yelling and cursing, and—can I be honest? I hope I do not have perfect holy-roly Christians reading this book like they have never made a mistake, or have never sinned in their life? I didn't think so. Anyway, I have to admit, as he kept yelling, I lost it and started yelling and cursing him back out. He eventually got quiet as if to be shocked that I lost it and stopped yelling. Probably was happy—well the enemy was. Afterwards it felt good giving him a piece of my mind. He got on my nerves, and I needed to let him know that I wasn't playing with him. But days later, God began to deal with me. He began to tell me that I knew better, and that I must love despite how people treat me and to watch what I say. I quickly repented. He showed me in his word that I must be quiet when the enemy is before me. *[Psalms 39:1]* So basically what God was ministering to me was that I should have stayed calm and that I did not have to sit up and argue with the enemy—someone who did not respect me. All I had to do was get away from that person and depart from evil. *[Psalms 37:27]* I have learned after going through so much stuff that it takes two to argue and two to fight. The enemy cannot and will not fight with himself. So I believe that is why God says in His word to resist the devil and he will flee. *[James 4:7]* If I would have just resisted and stayed calm and not yelled back with him, I would have passed the test. God knows that we cannot possibly be as perfect as He is, but we should strive for perfection. *[Matthew 5:48]* We strive to be more like God and this is why we have to ask God to cleanse us so that our spirit's can be clean daily. Remember, iron sharpens iron. *[Psalms 51:2, 51:10]* He's not talking about cleansing your body by taking a bath, although that wouldn't be bad…smiling….but He's talking about cleansing your spirit from everything that is not like Him. For example, cursing and full of a negative attitude, or drinking and getting drunk, or smoking drugs and taking pills, or even stealing from a store. When you do these things, this means that you need to be clean—spiritually clean. I can hear you asking the question, "How do I get clean?" Well, to answer your question, you get clean by first of all repenting of the sin that you are doing, ask God to forgive you, and then you ask God to take away that or those very things that you are struggling with as you surrender it to Him. Before you know it, you'll feel better and you will be set free from that or those things that had you bound.

God knows that we cannot possibly be as perfect as He is, but we should strive for perfection

---

7 DAY SERIES OF STUDY
"IRON SHARPENS IRON"

Name of Study:

Today's Date:

Focusing Scriptures:

7-DAY FAST 6AM-6PM

Eat only fruits and drink only water. You may eat soup no meats after 6pm. You will study and stand on the scriptures below by reading and confessing them daily.

MONDAY

STUDY THE CHAPTER ON THE WORD <u>REFINE</u>, WRITE OUT YOUR THOUGHTS ON THE SCRIPTURE FOR THE DAY AND HOW IT WILL HELP YOU AS YOU MOVE TOWARDS YOUR PURPOSE.

Zechariah 13:9

_____
_____
_____
_____
_____

TUESDAY

STUDY THE CHAPTER ON THE WORD <u>PRIDE</u>, WRITE OUT YOUR THOUGHTS ON THE SCRIPTURE FOR THE DAY AND HOW IT WILL HELP YOU AS YOU MOVE TOWARDS YOUR PURPOSE.

Proverbs 16:18

_____
_____
_____
_____
_____
_____
_____

WEDNESDAY

STUDY THE CHAPTER ON THE WORD <u>CLEANSE</u>, WRITE OUT YOUR THOUGHTS ON THE SCRIPTURE FOR THE DAY AND HOW IT WILL HELP YOU AS YOU MOVE TOWARDS YOUR PURPOSE.

Psalms 51:1-15

_____
_____
_____
_____
_____
_____
_____

Position Your Faith for Great Success 185

THURSDAY

STUDY THE CHAPTER ON THE WORD <u>DECEIVE</u>, WRITE OUT YOUR THOUGHTS ON THE SCRIPTURE FOR THE DAY AND HOW IT WILL HELP YOU AS YOU MOVE TOWARDS YOUR PURPOSE. GOD HAS GIVEN YOU POWER.

I John 1:8

_____
_____
_____
_____

FRIDAY

STUDY THE CHAPTER ON THE WORD <u>WILL</u>, WRITE OUT YOUR THOUGHTS ON THE SCRIPTURE FOR THE DAY AND HOW IT WILL HELP YOU AS YOU MOVE TOWARDS YOUR PURPOSE.

Psalms 50:15, Hebrews 13:21

_____
_____
_____
_____
_____
_____

SATURDAY

STUDY THE CHAPTER ON THE WORD <u>SHARPEN</u>, WRITE OUT YOUR THOUGHTS ON THE SCRIPTURE FOR THE DAY AND HOW IT WILL HELP YOU AS YOU MOVE TOWARDS YOUR PURPOSE.

I Samuel 13:20

SUNDAY

STUDY THE CHAPTER ON THE WORD <u>PERFECT</u>, WRITE OUT YOUR THOUGHTS ON THE SCRIPTURE FOR THE DAY AND HOW IT WILL HELP YOU AS YOU MOVE TOWARDS YOUR PURPOSE.

2 Samuel 22:31, James 1:4

LIST ALL OF THE AREAS IN YOUR LIFE WHERE YOU TALK TOO MUCH. WRITE DOWN THE NEGATIVE WORDS.

1.
2.
3.
4.
5.
6.
7.
8.
9.
10.

WRITE YOUR COMMITMENT ON HOW YOU PLAN TO WATCH WHAT YOU SAY AND CHANGE YOUR APPROACH AND ATTITUDE.

_____
_____
_____
_____
_____
_____

_____
_____
_____
_____
_____
_____
_____
_____

LIST ALL OF THE AREAS IN YOUR LIFE THAT YOU PLAN TO CHANGE THE NEGATIVE WAY YOU TALK AND ACT WHEN THE ENEMY IS BEFORE YOU.

1.

2.

3.

4.

5.

6.

7.

8.

9.

10.

***Purchase the Workbook for further study on this chapter*

8

Two Heads Are Better Than One

Two Heads Are Better Than One

I grew up taking care of my own business and minding my own business. It wasn't anything unusual when I had to do something myself because there was no one around to help me. I have always tried to take care of my own business by myself first before ever thinking about calling anyone. I was thinking, "I could just handle it myself." Little did I realize that I had friends and family around me ready to help. If we could handle everything on our own, we wouldn't need God, nor friends, nor family. The bible specifically tells us that "Two heads are better than one." *[Ecclesiastes 4:9]* Neither one of us on this God's green earth can do everything on our own. My mom always used to tell me, "Stephanie, you can't do everything on your own; you need to let somebody help you." Although she also taught me to be independent, but one thing she didn't teach me is to be proud. Pride comes in so many ways. Most people think pride is only when a person does not want to admit when they are wrong, but pride is also when you do not want anybody to help you that God has sent to help you. What you have to realize is that, when that particular person wanting to help you obey God, this is how they receive their blessing for the seed they sowed to help you in the first place. But when you do not allow them to help you, this hinders your blessing. You notice I did not say their blessing? Well, because when they obey God's command, they have already passed the test and the seed that they attempted to sow, will come back to them no matter if you obey or not. My mom's words helped me to realize that I couldn't do everything by myself. I guess I felt this way because, besides her help, I've had to do things all by myself. I took my mom's words and started allowing people to help me. My very dear friend is truly God sent. She's always there to lend a helping hand. But at times I do not allow her to help me. I am working on that. One thing you have to realize is that you cannot complete your purpose by yourself. God places people in your life to be a help to get you where you need to be. He wants to fulfill His purpose in you and through you. When God has assigned certain people to come into your life, be careful that you do not block them out; they will play a very important key piece in your life. Pushing them away will only set you back and delays your blessing that God has lined up for you. The devil will come to steal, kill, and to destroy *[John 10:10]* what God has planned for you and what those persons are to do. It is always important to stay in prayer at all times and wait for God's instructions on making decisions. The bible tells us to pray without ceasing. *[1 Thessalonians 5:17]* You should pray in such away—everyday that when the devil tries to come with his tricks and schemes, you can destroy his plans before they can ever manifest. God will never lead you astray. But you can lead yourself astray through disobedience. God will always send you a warning and He will always let you know whether it's Him or it's the devil. Some of the fiery darts that the devil brings are much too great for you to fight alone. That's why God will bring a prayer warrior/partner along with you to help you to fight. That person will have your back, without stabbing you in the back. You may ask, how will I know they're sent from God, trust me you will know, God says in His word to try the spirit by the spirit *[1 John 4:1]*, you can watch and discern what spirit they are operating in by watching how they talk and act—the things they say, their lifestyle; if they live by the word of God. This will tell you if they are sent from God. Also another way you can tell if they are sent from God is if their destiny lines up with your destiny. Does their future line up with your future? Is their plan the same as your plan in God? God will never put two people together and their destinies and plans do not match. He will always put you with someone who's going in the same direction you are. To my sisters, if Mr. Joe Blow is lazy, strung out on drugs, broke as a joke and jobless, you should immediately know he ain't the one for you. And to my brothers, if Ms. Sally Jane ain't got no job and ain't tryin' to get one, got fifteen kids, keep a filthy house, and got men coming in and out of her house, while at the same time saying they're only friends, I guarantee you she's not the one. This is for my sista's and my brotha's, if you have a friend that you think is sent from Heaven and they're jealous of you and your accomplishments, hatin' on you every time something good comes your way; they always have something negative to say, trust me they're not your friend and they are not from God. A friend that is sent from God is going to support you, rebuke you—tell you when you're wrong, love you, pray for you, read the bible with you, be there for you when you don't have nothing, pushes you to go higher and get better and always has your back, that is your friend and that is the one you should be with. God never makes mistakes. If God promised you a husband or a wife, or a friend, they may not come when you want them too, but they will come when God feels like you're ready for them. God will keep His promise.

God wants you to be happy. He wants you to be married if you so desire. This is why He created Adam and Eve. He created Eve to be a help-mate for Adam. They both are together. They both are one. Two heads are better than one. She compliments him, and he compliments her. But in order to receive the husband or wife for you, you must be physically, spiritually, and emotionally ready. Are you all of these things? God knows when you are ready and the same goes with receiving a God sent friend. You must be ready because if you are not, you will hurt them and ruin the assignment and the blessing that God has given to you.

Many times people jump into relationships too quick. This does not mean that the person that they were with were not the one, it just means that the person did not wait on God's instructions and they moved before God and allowed sin to come in and bring destruction. Now you two have to start all over again. This is why you two argue and fight all the time because you did not wait on God. Don't get in the flesh and do your own thing. This brings catastrophe, heartaches, torment, turmoil, and maybe even deadly outcomes. But if you always walk in the spirit and listen to God's instructions, you will always have peace, victorious relationships, and the wholesome connection needed to fulfill the purpose you two have been brought together to complete.

God will never lead you astray. He will always send you a warning and He will always let you know whether it's Him or the devil.

---

7 DAY SERIES OF STUDY
"TWO HEADS ARE BETTER THAN ONE"

Name of Study:
Today's Date:
Focusing Scriptures:

7-DAY FAST 6AM-6PM

Eat only fruits and drink only water. You may eat soup no meats after 6pm. You will study and stand on the scriptures below by reading and confessing them daily.

MONDAY

STUDY THE CHAPTER ON THE WORD <u>PURPOSE</u>, WRITE OUT YOUR THOUGHTS ON THE SCRIPTURE FOR THE DAY AND HOW IT WILL HELP YOU AS YOU MOVE TOWARDS YOUR PURPOSE.

Romans 8:28

_____
_____
_____
_____
_____
_____

TUESDAY

STUDY THE CHAPTER ON THE WORD <u>UNITY</u>, WRITE OUT YOUR THOUGHTS ON THE SCRIPTURE FOR THE DAY AND HOW IT WILL HELP YOU AS YOU MOVE TOWARDS YOUR PURPOSE.

Psalms 133:1

WEDNESDAY

STUDY THE CHAPTER ON THE WORD <u>LOVE</u>, WRITE OUT YOUR THOUGHTS ON THE SCRIPTURE FOR THE DAY AND HOW IT WILL HELP YOU AS YOU MOVE TOWARDS YOUR PURPOSE.

I John 3:18

THURSDAY

STUDY THE CHAPTER ON THE WORD JOY, WRITE OUT YOUR THOUGHTS ON THE SCRIPTURE FOR THE DAY AND HOW IT WILL HELP YOU AS YOU MOVE TOWARDS YOUR PURPOSE.

Galatians 5:22, Philippians 1:4

FRIDAY

STUDY THE CHAPTER ON THE WORD PEACE, WRITE OUT YOUR THOUGHTS ON THE SCRIPTURE FOR THE DAY AND HOW IT WILL HELP YOU AS YOU MOVE TOWARDS YOUR PURPOSE.

Isaiah 9:6

SATURDAY

STUDY THE CHAPTER ON THE WORD <u>COMMUNICATE</u>, WRITE OUT YOUR THOUGHTS ON THE SCRIPTURE FOR THE DAY AND HOW IT WILL HELP YOU AS YOU MOVE TOWARDS YOUR PURPOSE.

I Titus 6:13, Hebrews 13:16

SUNDAY

STUDY THE CHAPTER ON THE WORD <u>LISTEN</u>, WRITE OUT YOUR THOUGHTS ON THE SCRIPTURE FOR THE DAY AND HOW IT WILL HELP YOU AS YOU MOVE TOWARDS YOUR PURPOSE.

Isaiah 49:1, Psalms 143:1

LIST 10 AREAS IN YOUR LIFE WHERE YOU DO NOT ALLOW PEOPLE TO HELP OR TO BLESS YOU.

1.
2.
3.
4.
5.
6.
7.
8.
9.
10.

WRITE YOUR COMMITMENT ON HOW YOU PLAN NOT TO BE SELFISH AND ALLOW OTHERS TO HELP YOU OR BLESS YOU.

_____
_____
_____
_____
_____
_____

_____
_____
_____
_____
_____
_____
_____
_____
_____

LIST ALL OF THE AREAS IN YOUR LIFE THAT YOU PLAN TO CHANGE TOWARDS SHARING YOUR THINGS WITH OTHERS.

1.
2.
3.
4.
5.
6.
7.
8.
9.
10.

***Purchase the Workbook for further study on this chapter*

9

You Are Special Like the Cedar Tree

You Are Special Like the Cedar Tree

So many times we as people look one way on the outside but are a totally different person on the inside. We wear masks only to hide the real truth that lies within each one of us for the fear of everybody knowing the truth. We smile in each others face, but when we get home behind closed doors, the mask comes off and the real person that wishes she or he was dead comes out. I often wonder why this is so true. I have come to the conclusion that it's because we do not want people to judge us. We do not want the supposed to be Christians to judge us. We do not want people to look at us crazy. It's funny when I think about it, but what if all of our thoughts were exposed? What if everybody could see, read, and hear everyone of our thoughts? Many of us would be very embarrassed. Most, if not all of us, would run and hide and never come out. Sometimes we are the most judgmental human beings on this earth. We can make a person feel either beautiful, or we make them feel very ugly. We can make a person feel smart, or we can make them feel very dumb. We can make them feel special, or we can make them feel like the lowest person ever created. Words can cut a person into little bitty pieces until it shatters their life. I'm a living witness that words can scar you and shatter you for life. There were words, years ago, in my past that came and scared my future. If I believed their words and allowed them to stick to me, I would not be here today. I know there is someone who is reading this book that agrees. I was always a talented person, filled with muti-talents that God only trusted to give to me. At times I wondered why, but only He knows. But in my past I ran across people who could not receive the fact that God had blessed me the way that He did. They were very jealous, hating on my gifts, talents, the way I showed love towards everybody, and my personality that loves to have a lot of fun. Even though God had blessed me with these multi-talents and gifts, I still felt very lonely and unloved. I felt rejected and alone—like nobody cared. You ever felt like that? You may still feel this way. But one day as I grew closer to the Lord, and began to know His voice more clear; and established a deeper relationship with Him, He spoke these words to me with His powerful whispering voice, *"You are special to me......You are the apple of My eye."* I almost couldn't believe my ears. I could not believe that God would speak these words to me—but He did. At that moment I felt very special and very beautiful. It literally brought a smile to my face as it ignited my spirit. I believed God, and I knew His words were true because He doesn't lie. Man may lie all day long, but God never lies. He's the same yesterday, today, and forever more. *[Hebrews 13:8]* He doesn't say sweet words of love and encouragement and then come back and say something evil. As I was in consecration with the Lord, He led me to read

[Ezekiel 31: 1-9]. I believe if I can remember, I did not feel special because I was going through one of the most challenging times in the ministry and with some of the people in the church. I'm sure I'm not alone on this. I was down because it seemed as if no one wanted to hang around me nor did they want to have a conversation with me unless they wanted something like prayer, or wanted me to be a trash can and sit and listen to all of their dirt, or they wanted me to do something for them, or others were telling lies about me. I felt all alone and rejected. I did not realize that this was all about God's purpose. He was allowing this to happen against me for a greater purpose, but at the time I could not see it. All I could see was that they were attacks that the devil was bringing against me through people. Ever been in my shoes? Ever had or are having the same thing to happen to you? You are hated for doing a work for the Lord, or you are hated because God has blessed you with special gifts and talents? God really ministered to me and maybe this will minister to you as well. On this particular day God took me to these scriptures. He took me to the 31st chapter of Ezekiel, verses 1-9. The chapter talked about the parable of the cedar of Lebanon. God was talking to Ezekiel and telling him what to say to Pharaoh the King of Egypt and his multitude: who was he like in his greatness? Verses 1-9 read like this: *[1] And it came to pass in the eleventh year, in the third month, in the first day of the month, that the word of the Lord came unto me, saying. [2] Son of man, speak to Pharaoh King of Egypt, and to his multitude: Whom art*

thou like in thy greatness? [3] Behold, the Assyrian was a cedar in Lebanon with fair branches, and with a shadowing shroud, and of an high stature; and his top was among the thick boughs. [4] The waters made him great, the deep set him up on high with her rivers running round about his plants, and sent out her little rivers unto all the trees of the field. [5] Therefore his height was exalted above all the trees of the field, and his boughs were multiplied, and his branches became long because of the multitude of waters, when he shot forth. [6] All the fowls of heaven made their nests in his boughs, and under his branches did all the beasts of the field bring forth their young, and under his shadow dwelt all great nations. [7] "Thus was he fair in his greatness, in the length of his branches: for his root was by great waters." [8] "The cedars in the garden of God could not hide him: the fir trees were not like his boughs, and the chestnut trees were not like his branches; nor any tree in the garden of God was like unto him in his beauty." [9] "I have made him fair by the multitude of his branches: so that all the trees of Eden that were in the garden of God, envied him." As I read those verses, verse 4 hit something within me when it said: *"The waters made him great,"* It was not that he was great, but the watering of the WATER is what made him great. God was his water. God said in His word in *[John 7:38]* that: *"He that believeth on me, as the scripture hath said, out of his belly shall flow rivers of living water." Kjv.* Which means that out of our bellies shall flow rivers of God's Agape Spirit—His Agape love which makes the tears run down our faces like a river that flows constantly down a step hill. And then He also said in *[Matthew 5:6]* "...*they that hunger and thirst after righteousness shall be filled."* If you hunger to live right, treat your neighbor right, live by God's word and His promises, you shall be filled. Filled with what? Filled with God's precious Holy Spirit. In these few verses He said that: *"the deep set him up on high with her rivers running round about his plants, and sent out her little rivers unto all the trees of the field."* The word of the Lord was saying this to me. God set him high above all of the other plants, that the water that flowed all over him. The little left over ran over the rest of them. And this is what God is doing for you. He has highly favored you. He has set you above all of the rest. He spoke these words to me, *"You are special, and this is why they envy you."* I am so grateful that God would first find me special, then highly favor me above all of the rest. This is what God has done for you. He has highly favored you and made you stand out above all of the rest. You are chosen. Many are called, but few are chosen. [Matthew 22: 14] This is your faith—faith to trust that in those times when it seems as if you are all alone and nobody is on your side, and nobody cares, it's just a set up to reposition your faith towards heaven; which is your trust that if God be for you, He's more than all those *(the world)* that are against you. When you are chasing after purpose, you are not chasing after people. If you chase after people and what people think, you will get lost and off focused. God has not sent you here to be a people chaser, but God has sent you here to be a God chaser. This is your success! When you are chasing after God, you may have to walk alone at times. No one may not like you. They may not understand you. They may not receive you. The may say all manner of evil against you, but just keep on walking and doing what God has called you to do. Just keep on walking towards your success. Like the word of the Lord says, shake the dust from your feet and keep on walking *[Luke 9:5]*. Amen? Praise God. I feel you're victorious today from my testimony and from these words. Grab a hold of it and don't let go, you're release is on the way! Praise God!

When you are chasing after purpose, you are not chasing after people.

People will make you miss what God has planned for you. When you are chasing after your purpose, you are not chasing after people. When you chase after people, you will be led in the wrong direction. They will get you off focus, and you are worse off than you were before you made the mistake in allowing them to lead you in the first place. It is very important to get delivered from people, if you allow them to control your future and lead you, you will eventually crash and be destroyed. Only God can lead you to a prosperous future. Only God can lead you to a purposed driven—God filled future. He can work out every situation that you may be going through right now. Please, no matter how hard it gets to follow what God has purposed for you to do in this life, please do not turn to a humanistic source—people who are human just like you. But turn to the Lord who cares and loves you; and is waiting to lead you towards a victorious, prosperous, and healthy future. When you are going through, it may seem as if God is against you and do not want you to make it, or wants to see you broke with no money and no job, or He's just sitting back watching people hate on you and say all manner of evil against you and won't do anything about it, just know that God is with you. It's not in the way you can see it right now, but He is. God is positioning, He's pushing, He's tugging, and He's pulling your faith for great success for your future—which is the purpose He has already laid out for you. Can you agree to this? I sure can! Thank you Jesus that You still care about us and are concerned about everything we care about and are going through!

I have learned by watching trees or plants that they need water to grow. They need water for minerals, and vitamins, and nourishment. If trees or plants do not get these proper things, they will eventually wither up and die. This is just like us, if we do not read the word of God, allow Him to speak to us, feed us through His word, or bath us in His spirit, we will eventually wither up and die. I am not saying that our earthly bodies will die, but our spiritual bodies will die. This is why we turn away from God and do those things that God is so against and has already delivered us out of. For example, you may get back on drugs, go on an alcohol drinking frenzy, or get into perverted life styles because your spiritual bodies have withered away. But thank God we have an advocate that speaks constantly to the Father that sits on His right side, who's making intercession for us daily, and His name is Jesus Christ *[1 John 2:1-2]*. Thank God that He died just for that very thing that you are struggling with. Through His suffering and great sacrifice; it should give you the conviction and the will to repent and turn from those lifestyles and habits that is keeping you in bondage. Verse [5] in that same chapter says: that *"Therefore his height was exalted above all the trees of the field, and his boughs were multiplied, and his branches became long because of the multitude of waters, when he shot forth."* This is clearly saying that when you allow God to flow freely in you and through you, He will exalt you above everybody else. He said in *[Matthew 23:12] "that whosoever shall exalt himself shall be abased, and he that shall humble himself shall be exalted."* The more you humble yourself and know that you are special—singled out and called out by God, God will raise you higher and higher.

Back in verse 5, God's Spirit—which is the living water, was nourishing him and providing the vitamins needed for growth, and minerals needed for energy when he got weak, it allowed the tree to multiply. When you get weak and you feel as though you can't go any further, God will provide you with multitudes of water so that every limb, every part of your body/spirit will get what it needs to multiply. Before the multiplying comes, it can be very hard and sometimes unbearable, because you can not see the change in the flow of the water and you can not see the full vision of what God is doing in you. You're just looking at all the hell that's going on in your life that only satan has sent. Well, this is not always true, there are times when God has to take you through, to bring you out. He takes you through your dry land and brings you over the Red Sea with the VICTORY! Hallelujah! That's great news to know how special you are that God would even choose you to be special. I love God so much. He is so awesome and there is truly no one like Him. In verses [8-9] it says: *"The cedars in the garden of God could not hide him: the fir trees were not like his boughs, and the chestnut trees were not like his branches; nor any tree in the garden of God was like unto him in his beauty."* [9] *"I have made him fair by the multitude of his branches: so that all the trees of Eden that were in the garden of God, envied him."* I want to give you some great news, that when God begins to bless you, no one will be able to hide God's greatness in you, they will not be able to hide the great anointing that's on your life, they will not be able to hide the great ministry that God is building in you, they will not be able to speak against what God is doing in your life and in your family. Their jealousy will not be able to fester and cause all kinds of embarrassment. God will arise. He will arise in you and each one of your enemies will be scattered. The bible says, *"Let God arise, let his enemies be scattered...."* [Psalms 68:1] God will arise in your situation and in your life and all of your enemies will be scattered. You will be able to stand on your two feet and tell how God brought you out, how he delivered you, and how He healed you to a greater glory and a greater testimony.

You can not forget that water also purges. Water breaks up everything that's not like him. So all that is not like God inside of you, is broken up and purged out so that you can be more like God.

Thank God that He died just for that very thing that you are struggling with.

---

7 DAY SERIES OF STUDY
"YOU ARE SPECIAL LIKE THE CEDAR TREE"

Name of Study:
Today's Date:
Focusing Scriptures:

7-DAY FAST 6AM-6PM

Eat only fruits and drink only water. You may eat soup no meats after 6pm. You will study and stand on the scriptures below by reading and confessing them daily.

MONDAY

STUDY THE CHAPTER ON THE WORD <u>CEDAR TREE</u>, WRITE OUT YOUR THOUGHTS ON THE SCRIPTURE FOR THE DAY AND HOW IT WILL HELP YOU AS YOU MOVE TOWARDS YOUR PURPOSE.

Psalm 92:12

_____
_____
_____
_____
_____
_____

TUESDAY

STUDY THE CHAPTER ON THE WORD <u>UNITY</u>, WRITE OUT YOUR THOUGHTS ON THE SCRIPTURE FOR THE DAY AND HOW IT WILL HELP YOU AS YOU MOVE TOWARDS YOUR PURPOSE.

Psalms 133:1

_____
_____
_____
_____
_____
_____
_____

WEDNESDAY

STUDY THE CHAPTER ON THE WORD <u>LOVE</u>, WRITE OUT YOUR THOUGHTS ON THE SCRIPTURE FOR THE DAY AND HOW IT WILL HELP YOU AS YOU MOVE TOWARDS YOUR PURPOSE.

I John 3:18

_____
_____
_____
_____
_____
_____
_____

THURSDAY

STUDY THE CHAPTER ON THE WORD JOY, WRITE OUT YOUR THOUGHTS ON THE SCRIPTURE FOR THE DAY AND HOW IT WILL HELP YOU AS YOU MOVE TOWARDS YOUR PURPOSE.

Galatians 5:22, Philippians 1:4

FRIDAY

STUDY THE CHAPTER ON THE WORD PEACE, WRITE OUT YOUR THOUGHTS ON THE SCRIPTURE FOR THE DAY AND HOW IT WILL HELP YOU AS YOU MOVE TOWARDS YOUR PURPOSE.

Isaiah 9:6

SATURDAY

STUDY THE CHAPTER ON THE WORD <u>COMMUNICATE</u>, WRITE OUT YOUR THOUGHTS ON THE SCRIPTURE FOR THE DAY AND HOW IT WILL HELP YOU AS YOU MOVE TOWARDS YOUR PURPOSE.

I Titus 6:13, Hebrews 13:16

SUNDAY

STUDY THE CHAPTER ON THE WORD <u>LISTEN</u>, WRITE OUT YOUR THOUGHTS ON THE SCRIPTURE FOR THE DAY AND HOW IT WILL HELP YOU AS YOU MOVE TOWARDS YOUR PURPOSE.

Isaiah 49:1, Psalms 143:1

LIST 10 SPECIAL THINGS ABOUT YOURSELF.

1.
2.
3.
4.
5.
6.
7.
8.
9.
10.

WRITE YOUR COMMITMENTS ON HOW YOU PLAN TO COMPLIMENT SOMEONE ELSE ON HOW SPECIAL THEY ARE. IF YOU HAVE ALREADY DONE IT, WHAT DID THEY SAY?

_____
_____
_____
_____
_____
_____

_____
_____
_____
_____
_____
_____
_____

LIST HOW YOU PLAN TO CHANGE THE WAY YOU FEEL ABOUT YOURSELF. THESE AREAS MAY BE NEGATIVE OR POSITIVE.

1.

2.

3.

4.

5.

6.

7.

8.

9.

10.

***Purchase the Workbook for further study on this chapter*

10

Don't Judge A Book by its Cover

Don't Judge A Book by its Cover

Judging a book by its cover is easy when you are looking at it from the outside and NOT from the inside. You can easily judge what you think that book is about, but when you open it up and read the facts, you'll find that your judgment was all wrong. Ever been there? Ever had someone to judge you from what they thought they saw on the outside and you knew that what they were judging about you were all wrong? I understand your hurt and your anger because I've been there. You may be still there. I can tell you that it doesn't feel good, but you can overcome it and move on.

One of the hurts I have experienced was church hurt in my life and ministry. While dealing with my situation, I felt all alone and wanted to give up, feeling as though nobody cared, but through time, healing, and being able to forgive, I was able to move on with my life. You may be experiencing this in your life right now. You would love to give those who hurt you a piece of your mind, but I say to you, and you may not want to receive this but it's true. You must forgive them and move on. You must release the hurt from church hurt or what ever hurt you have experienced. You cannot look at the people because it is not the people, but it's the devil operating in them to bring you down. You have to understand that God allows what He wants to allow to happen to you—whether in the church or out of the church. If God is allowing this or has allowed this to happen against you, it's for your good. It is birthing your purpose from the pain of your past and bringing you into a place of victorious peace. Your peace, in this, comes as a center piece of no matter what people say, if God is for you, He's more than all those that are against you. Since then, the Lord has blessed me with a brand new faith and a new hope to know that if I just keep my eyes on the Him, He's going to bless me with more, no matter what people say. I was committed, faithful, and obedient to what God had told me to do. I have learned that there are times when following what God tells you to do does not always look right to some people, but do not worry about what people say, and what they may attempt to do to you, God always has an expected end for you. He will never allow your enemies to trample over you. He will never set you up for embarrassment. If God can and is doing it for me, He can do it for you. God wants His people to have great success. He wants your future to soar. He wants you to be on top and not at the bottom. Although it looks as if you're at the bottom right now, I want you to know that your time is coming. You are about to go to the top. You are about to have an **AND SUDDENLY EXPERIENCE**. God is on the way with your blessing AND READY TO GIVE IT TO YOU AND SUDDENLY *(2 Chronicles 29:35-36)*. But you must believe and keep your faith; it's all on the way.

You are about to have an **AND SUDDENLY EXPERIENCE**. God is on the way with your blessing AND READY TO GIVE IT TO YOU AND SUDDENLY

One thing I have learned is that God will never give up on you. You may give up on yourself, and others may give up on you because of what they see you going through, but GOD WILL NEVER GIVE UP ON YOU. If God made you a promise, He will and is obligated to fulfill it. The great news is that He wants to fulfill it. I know the devil is trying to tell you all kinds of lies like, "God lied to you, look at you your daughter/son is in jail and is supposed to be in church, saved, and living for God. You're a no good for nothing unfit parent, look at your daughter she's pregnant at thirteen, God killed your baby and you'll never have anymore children, you're broke with no money and will never get off of food stamps, they hate you on your job because you're fat and you're too lazy and stupid—you're a suck-up to the supervisor that's how you made it to the top. The devil is telling you all of these lies and many more, but do not listen to him, he's the father of lies and he's supposed to lie to you and make you believe that you're a failure, you'll never amount to anything, and the rest of the lies that he is telling you—even the ones he's saying in your ears as you read this book right now. DO NOT LISTEN

TO HIM. He's lying to you! Rebuke him and command him to leave you alone by the precious and powerful Name of Jesus Christ. Tell him that the Blood of Jesus Christ is against him and his lies. You are victorious and that you are somebody, God is a forgiver of mistakes and sins, you are beautiful and not ugly, you do have a future, you are a great mother, father, son, daughter, step-son, step-daughter, adopted daughter, adopted son, sister, brother, friend, grandmother, grandfather, granddaughter, grandson, niece, nephew, and so much more in Jesus name.

Say and declare this out loud everyday until it, by faith, gets down in you, manifests in your life, and you have complete victory in these areas:

"I DECLARE AND DECREE ON THIS DAY OF _____ THE _____st/nd//rd/th year of _____, THAT I AM VICTORIOUS IN EVERY AREA OF MY LIFE! I BELIEVE THAT MY DAY WILL NOT MAKE ME BOUND TO SATAN'S LIES, AND WILL NOT MAKE ME STOOP TO HIS EVIL LEVEL. I WILL SUCCEED, NO ONE CAN STOP ME, NO ONE CAN HINDER ME, NO ONE CAN CHANGE THE BLESSINGS THAT GOD HAS FOR ME TODAY, IN JESUS NAME, AMEN."

Say this everyday until it becomes apart of your life. Do not be afraid of walking and living a life of success. Sometimes we as people think that when things are going good, evil or wrong is right around the corner; and so we look for it, we wait for it like it's supposed to happen. But what you have to realize is that we as believers are supposed to have a life of success. Our lives are supposed to be full of peace, full of joy, full of success, full of blessings and favor. We are not supposed to be going through. We are not supposed to be without; we are not supposed to be beat down and defeated. You are an over-comer. I am not saying that there are not going to be days that are challenging, and days that are almost at times too much to bear. But there again, God promises in His word that He will not put more on us than what we can bear. Take hold of your future! Reposition your faith for greatness for your future! God has so much in-store for you that's why He's left you an unchangeable guide—the Holy Bible to help you along this life when challenges arise. That doesn't mean give up, but what it merely means is to get on your knees, take God at His word, and believe Him for everything that He has promised you, your family (husband—wife—son—daughter), your friends, your ministry, and for your own life. Amen? Amen.

The outcome of being judged was awesome! I couldn't say this back then, but I can say this now because I have gotten the victory over it. The reason why I can tell you not to give up especially when you give up on yourself, is because God never gave up on me. They judged me from what they thought they saw on the outside, but never got to know who I really was and what was really going on the inside of my life—my book. This is why it is very important not to "judge a book by its cover" because almost every time you'll be wrong. And you never know, that person just may be the one who will have to help you one day. Be very careful how you treat people because you may be entertaining angels unaware *[Hebrews 13:1-2]*. You should get to know a person for who they are, and accept them for who they are. We all are supposed to love one another *[Hebrews 13:2]*, not tear one another down. The bible says for us to *esteem one another higher than we esteem ourselves [Philippians 2:3]*. If you are not living a life of loving others and esteeming others higher than you esteem yourself, then start today. Your life will start to bloom with joy, peace, love, and happiness.

Get to know a person for who they are, and accept them for who they are.

Make this day a day that you will go back to every person that you have judged, and tell them that you are sorry for judging them. Call, write, email, text, do what ever you have to do to get it straight with that person or those persons. This is what makes you an honest and true man, woman, and youth of God and people will respect you for doing this—especially God. I believe that this will mend back what the devil meant to tare a part in the first place. God is calling a people who all they care about is pleasing Him, being real, and honest with who they are and keeping peace with one another.

7 DAY SERIES OF STUDY
"DON'T JUDGE A BOOK BY ITS COVER"

Name of Study:
Today's Date:
Focusing Scriptures:

7-DAY FAST 6AM-6PM

Eat only fruits and drink only water. You may eat soup no meats after 6pm. You will study and stand on the scriptures below by reading and confessing them daily.

MONDAY

STUDY THE CHAPTER ON THE WORD JUDGE, WRITE OUT YOUR THOUGHTS ON THE SCRIPTURE FOR THE DAY AND HOW IT WILL HELP YOU AS YOU MOVE TOWARDS YOUR PURPOSE.

Psalm 75:7

_____
_____
_____
_____
_____
_____

TUESDAY

STUDY THE CHAPTER ON THE WORD JUDGE, WRITE OUT YOUR THOUGHTS ON THE SCRIPTURE FOR THE DAY AND HOW IT WILL HELP YOU AS YOU MOVE TOWARDS YOUR PURPOSE.

James 5:9

_____
_____
_____
_____
_____
_____
_____

WEDNESDAY

STUDY THE CHAPTER ON THE WORD HELPS, WRITE OUT YOUR THOUGHTS ON THE SCRIPTURE FOR THE DAY AND HOW IT WILL HELP YOU AS YOU MOVE TOWARDS YOUR PURPOSE.

I Corinthians 12:28

_____
_____
_____
_____
_____
_____
_____

THURSDAY

STUDY THE CHAPTER ON THE WORD <u>STRIFE</u>, WRITE OUT YOUR THOUGHTS ON THE SCRIPTURE FOR THE DAY AND HOW IT WILL HELP YOU AS YOU MOVE TOWARDS YOUR PURPOSE.

Philippians 2:3

_____
_____
_____
_____
_____

FRIDAY

STUDY THE CHAPTER ON THE WORD <u>STRIFE</u>, WRITE OUT YOUR THOUGHTS ON THE SCRIPTURE FOR THE DAY AND HOW IT WILL HELP YOU AS YOU MOVE TOWARDS YOUR PURPOSE.

James 3:16

_____
_____
_____
_____
_____
_____

SATURDAY

STUDY THE CHAPTER ON THE WORD <u>HEALING</u>, WRITE OUT YOUR THOUGHTS ON THE SCRIPTURE FOR THE DAY AND HOW IT WILL HELP YOU AS YOU MOVE TOWARDS YOUR PURPOSE.

Isaiah 53:5

SUNDAY

STUDY THE CHAPTER ON THE WORD <u>HEALED</u>, WRITE OUT YOUR THOUGHTS ON THE SCRIPTURE FOR THE DAY AND HOW IT WILL HELP YOU AS YOU MOVE TOWARDS YOUR PURPOSE.

Psalms 107:20

LIST 10 HEALING STRATEGIES THAT YOU WILL USE NOT TO JUDGE THOSE WHO HAVE HURT YOU.

1.
2.
3.
4.
5.
6.
7.
8.
9.
10.

LIST AREAS IN YOUR LIFE WHERE YOU NEED HEALING WITH JUDGING OTHERS.

_____
_____
_____
_____
_____
_____
_____

LIST SCRIPTURES ON HEALING AND APPLY THEM TO YOUR HEALING LIST ABOVE AND SPEAK—CONFESS THEM DAILY.

1.
2.
3.
4.
5.
6.
7.
8.
9.
10.

***Purchase the Workbook for further study on this chapter*

11

The Potter and the Clay

The Potter and the Clay

When you think of a potter and a piece of clay you think of something having power over the other. As you read the bible it is obvious to know that the Potter has ownership over the piece of clay. Who is the Potter? The Potter is the Lord, and who is the piece of clay? The piece of clay is us human beings. The Potter is trying to create something from a lump of clay that has no form, into a master piece. What I am trying to say is that God is trying to make each and every one of us into something beautiful to look at—from the inside out. Which one would you rather look at, a beautiful work of art, trash in a dumpster, or a form that has no shape? I believe you'll quickly choose the work of art. This is what God is trying to do with you. He wants you to be beautiful to look at. He doesn't want you stinky and smelly or a form that nobody can make out what you are, He wants you as a sweet odor—a sweet smell in His nostrils. *[Philippians 4:18]* He wants you beautiful to look at from the inside out, and the outside in. This is His purpose to shape, make, and mold you into His own image; which means He has to get into you and mash out all of those things that are keeping you from looking, acting, sounding, and smelling like Him. If you are going to represent

Him, you have got to be just like Him. That is not always an easy thing to do. It is not easy to allow God to mash you up into His image. Why? Because it hurts too bad. There are too many changes you have to go through. These are the things you say. If you realize something, it does not take God long to do what He wants to do in all of us. What takes long is the fact that we fight His will for our lives. We fight God's purpose and plan for our lives. We fight the fact that while God is changing, forming, and cleansing us, by the fact that it hurts and it's by the fact that it's uncomfortable. I can hear you asking, "Please explain what you are saying?" Well, what I am saying is that as God changes, forms, and cleanses you, He is basically developing your character, your love, your mind, your heart, your life style, the choices you make that are not good choices, and so much more. While He is doing this, it doesn't always feel good. This is when it hurts and it's uncomfortable. He does a head to toe make over.

Synopsis:

Get a blank sheet of paper and a pencil or pen and draw a stick figure of a human. Depending on how talented you are in this area, you may be somewhat more creative with drawing your human form. But if you are a little challenged in this area (smile), all you need to do is make a simple stick figure of a round circled head, a long vertical line for the neck, chest, and stomach area. On this same drawing, draw a small heart on top of the chest area. Then draw two long diagonal lines. One going outward to the right, and the other going outward to the left for the left and right arms. Draw two longer lines for the left and right legs; and draw a small chart beside it and create the person that you are now. Do not worry if you have more bad things about yourself than good because when you create your new person underneath it, you will look much better. Try it, this will allow you to see those areas that you need and want to change about yourself. Look at the example and hopefully you'll get a better idea of what I am showing you with the sample below.

MY EXAMPLE OF THE PERSON I AM THAT NEEDS TO CHANGE:

EXAMPLE A:

> **MY HEAD:** *My thoughts are not good thoughts.*
>
> *-I'm thinking about all of these bills I have to pay, etc.*
>
> **MY HEART:** *has unforgiveness, hurt, malice, and strife because _____ hurt me, I can't forgive.*
>
> **MY ARMS:** *I used them to fight _____ the other day.*
>
> **MY FEET:** I kicked _____ for *talking bad about me.*
>
> *I use them for negative reasons.*

MY EXAMPLE OF THE PERSON THAT GOD IS CHANGING ME TO BE:

EXAMPLE B:

MY HEAD: *My thoughts are good thoughts that pleases the Lord.*
-I'm thinking about how I trust God to pay my bills, etc.
MY HEART: *Has forgiveness, love, and joy because I have released and let go of my past.*
MY ARMS: *I use them to hug and to show love towards everyone.*
MY FEET: *Will go only in places that are positive and not Negative, therefore I am blessed.*

Now you do your own EXAMPLE A and B. For Example A, take a clean sheet of paper and draw the human form either in your own artistic way, or in the stick figure that I have done on the previous page. Also, do not forget to add the chart with it so that you can write out the person you are right now that needs to change. Then for EXAMPLE B, draw another human form either in your artistic way, or in the stick figure that I have done on the previous page; and add the chart so that you can write out the person that God is changing you to be.

Here is a blank sample of what your EXAMPLE A AND B should look like.

EXAMPLE A:

MY HEAD:

MY HEART:

MY ARMS:

MY FEET:

EXAMPLE B:

MY HEAD:
MY HEART:
MY ARMS:
MY FEET:

7 DAY SERIES OF STUDY
"THE POTTER AND THE CLAY"

Name of Study:
Today's Date:
Focusing Scriptures:

7-DAY FAST 6AM-6PM

Eat only fruits and drink only water. You may eat soup no meats after 6pm. You will study and stand on the scriptures below by reading and confessing them daily.

MONDAY

STUDY THE CHAPTER ON THE WORD <u>DELIVERANCE</u>, WRITE OUT YOUR THOUGHTS ON THE SCRIPTURE FOR THE DAY AND HOW IT WILL HELP YOU AS YOU MOVE TOWARDS YOUR PURPOSE.

Psalm 32:7

_____
_____
_____
_____
_____
_____

TUESDAY

STUDY THE CHAPTER ON THE WORD <u>NEW</u>, WRITE OUT YOUR THOUGHTS ON THE SCRIPTURE FOR THE DAY AND HOW IT WILL HELP YOU AS YOU MOVE TOWARDS YOUR PURPOSE.

2 Corinthians 5:17

_____
_____
_____
_____
_____
_____
_____

WEDNESDAY

STUDY THE CHAPTER ON THE WORD <u>NEW</u>, WRITE OUT YOUR THOUGHTS ON THE SCRIPTURE FOR THE DAY AND HOW IT WILL HELP YOU AS YOU MOVE TOWARDS YOUR PURPOSE.

John 13:34

_____
_____
_____
_____
_____
_____
_____

THURSDAY

STUDY THE CHAPTER ON THE WORD <u>CLEANSE</u>, WRITE OUT YOUR THOUGHTS ON THE SCRIPTURE FOR THE DAY AND HOW IT WILL HELP YOU AS YOU MOVE TOWARDS YOUR PURPOSE.

Leviticus 16:30

FRIDAY

STUDY THE CHAPTER ON THE WORD <u>FORM</u>, WRITE OUT YOUR THOUGHTS ON THE SCRIPTURE FOR THE DAY AND HOW IT WILL HELP YOU AS YOU MOVE TOWARDS YOUR PURPOSE.

Titus 3:5

SATURDAY

STUDY THE CHAPTER ON THE WORD <u>CHANGE</u>, WRITE OUT YOUR THOUGHTS ON THE SCRIPTURE FOR THE DAY AND HOW IT WILL HELP YOU AS YOU MOVE TOWARDS YOUR PURPOSE.

Proverbs 24:21

SUNDAY

STUDY THE CHAPTER ON THE WORD <u>SIN</u>, WRITE OUT YOUR THOUGHTS ON THE SCRIPTURE FOR THE DAY AND HOW IT WILL HELP YOU AS YOU MOVE TOWARDS YOUR PURPOSE.

James 4:17

LIST 10 OF YOUR STRUGGLES THAT YOU NEED TO BE DELIVERED FROM.

1.
2.
3.
4.
5.
6.
7.
8.
9.
10.

LIST HOW YOU PLAN TO CHANGE THE WAY YOU FEEL ABOUT YOURSELF. THESE AREAS MAY BE NEGATIVE OR POSITIVE.

_____
_____
_____
_____
_____
_____

_____

_____

_____

_____

_____

_____

_____

LIST 10 OF YOUR STRUGGLES THAT YOU ARE GOING TO WORK ON CHANGING THIS YEAR.

1.
2.
3.
4.
5.
6.
7.
8.
9.
10.

***Purchase the Workbook for further study on this chapter*

12

I Am All That God Says I Am

I Am All That God Says I Am

Saying the words "I am all that God says I am" can be very challenging at times to believe especially when life's struggles, trials, and tribulations; and negative words of people come to make you forget. Those words will make you soon forget that you are all that God says that you are—special. God specifically tells you this in His word that you are special and that no one can be like you *[Deuteronomy 7:6]*. He also says in *[Jeremiah 29: 11-13]* that He knows the thoughts that He thinks of you, thoughts of good/peace, and not of evil, to give you an expected end. What this simply means is that the negative thoughts that you think of yourself, or the suicidal thoughts you think of yourself, or the fact that you feel that you are a failure and nobody loves or cares about you are not the thoughts that God thinks of you. God never gives up on us, we may give up on Him, but He never gives up on us. It says in *[Hebrews 13: 5]* No matter how bad how it may be in your life right now, God still has not forsaken you. Your future may seem very dim, but God will resurrect your future. He will come in the mist of your situation and quickly turn it around for your good. The awesome thing about that is the fact that you will win—you will come out with the victory. **God takes what seems like a defeated situation, and turn it**

around to a resurrection experience. There is a perfect example for this revelation. Let's look at the scripture in the book of *[John 11:1-16, 43]*. It talks about a man named Lazarus, Mary's brother, who was very sick and died, and the fact that when Jesus stepped on the scene, where he was, after being dead for four days, *[verse 17]* Lazarus was raised from the dead <u>immediately</u>. Lazarus' future seemed very dim. In the natural it looked as if his life was over and no chance of fulfilling God's plan for his life, especially after being dead for four whole days. But when Jesus came into the room, the defeated situation changed into a **resurrection experience** and Lazarus was raised from the dead. This may be what you are going through. Many people have given up on you because you don't have a job right now, or you don't have car to get around, or you may have a made the biggest mistake of your life by having a baby at fourteen, or you may be in rehab recovering from a bad accident without any chance of walking again, or in rehab for drugs or alcohol and it looks as if you'll never recover from what seem like a defeated situation. You need to ask yourself this question, *"Can my dry bones come back to life and live?"* Now after you have just asked yourself that question, now answer it by saying, *"Yes my dry bones WILL come back to life and live."* You can make it. God never looks at your now situation, He looks at your latter situation. *[Haggai 2:9]* He is saying in your situation right now, He knows where you are right now and He has made plans to bless you and to increase you. Your latter days shall be greater than your former days. Do not give up. He knows it's hard for you right now, but do not give up. He will fulfill His promise to you. *[Will be explained more in depth in the next chapter]* Ask yourself this question, *"Can I come out of my defeated attitude and dim situation, and get myself together and start believing that I, myself, and all that I am going through can be resurrected immediately just like Lazarus?"* Now answer, "yes". I believe with you.

---

*God takes what seems like a defeated situation,
and turn it around to a resurrection experience.*

One important thing I did not mention in John 11 that I cannot pass up. First of all after Jesus heard that Lazarus was dead, the bible says in verse 4 that he said to Mary and Martha, *"… This sickness is not unto death, but for the glory of God, that the Son of God might be glorified thereby."* This is showing that Jesus already knew that Lazarus would be raised from the dead, that he was going to be alright, and that God would be glorified. This is what God is doing in your, what seem like detrimental situation. He already knows what you are going through and He has already made plans to get you out of that situation, but He has to allow you to go through it in order that you'll share your testimony of how He brought you out it so that He can be glorified. God cannot get the glory in your life unless you go through something that will allow Him to get the glory. It doesn't mean that you have to get sick or something drastic or dramatic has to happen, no, actually something good can happen but even in the mist of that, God wants you to give Him the glory so that others will see how powerful He really is. Without God nothing is possible. With God, nothing is impossible. Do you receive that? I sure hope so.   One more point I want to make in this same chapter. The bible says in verse 6 that when Jesus heard that Lazarus was sick, he stayed where he was for two days because his faith was doubtless. He never doubted that Lazarus would be raised from the dead with a chance to live again. God is not doubting your situation; He's already made plans to bring you out with the victory. Here's another powerful encouragement for you. Starting in verse 21, Martha said to Jesus that if He had been there, her brother would not have died. Then in verse 23, Jesus said back to her that her brother will rise again. Then in verse 24, Martha comes back and says that she know that he will rise again in the resurrection at the last day. Jesus quickly said back to her, **"I am the resurrection and the life...He that believeth in me....shall he live."** Here is the revelation to all of this, God is the only One who can resurrect your situation. He is the only one that can help you get your life back and get back on your feet and live again. He is the resurrection—He is your rebirth, He is your renewal, He is your restoration, He is your revival, He is your new life, He is your getting up from your dead situation and your coming out and live again. God is your everything. You must believe this. This is the only way you will be able to come out and be delivered. This is the only way God can and will help you and turn your situation around.

You must believe that you are all that God says that you are no matter if no one ever tells you. Many times we look for people's approval. When you are doing a work for God, you may never get an approval, or a word of encouragement. This is how the devil has come to steal from God's people — through our praise for one another. He has stolen the fact that God has called us to esteem one another higher than our own selves *[Philippians 2:3, I Thessalonians 5:13]*. We should love and encourage each other. If you say you are a Christian, you should be ready to build your brother or your sister in Christ up and not tear them down. This is where the church lacks this. In this day and time the church is the last place a sinner wants to go to because of horror stories about sinners getting treated like nobodies, or nasty people because of their current lifestyles, or how they look or smell and it's not right. There are some churches, not all, have judged so hard and have been so cold hearted instead of showing love to everybody, that many Christians and sinners have gone back to the lifestyle they were living before they tried to come to the temple where God is supposed to be. Some churches are so full of pride and have such cold-hearted hearts that some people have literally given up. I believe God is not pleased with this. It grieves Him to see this in the church. I believe that God is coming to clean up his churches—the churches that He has called. God is on a mission to win back the souls that have been lost or have been badly damaged by the root of demonic and evil activity and attitudes. God loves His people too much to allow the devil to operate in people and loose the little salvation they had in trying to get their lives together and live for the Lord. I am certainly not bashing the church, I thank God for the churches that are doing the will of God, but for those that are not must get it right because God is coming back for a church without spot or wrinkle. *[Ephesians 5:27]* We as God's children have to love one another, accept one another no matter what our pasts, lifestyles, or struggles are/were; and come together as the bible says and win back what rightfully belongs to us and the church of God.

You are all that God says you are. Always remember, do not put your trust in man because man may fail you, but God will never fail you He will do just what He has promised. *[Joshua 23:14]*

7 DAY SERIES OF STUDY
"I AM ALL THAT GOD SAYS I AM"

Name of Study:
Today's Date:
Focusing Scriptures:

7-DAY FAST 6AM-6PM

Eat only fruits and drink only water. You may eat soup no meats after 6pm. You will study and stand on the scriptures below by reading and confessing them daily.

MONDAY

STUDY THE CHAPTER ON THE WORD <u>LOVED</u>, WRITE OUT YOUR THOUGHTS ON THE SCRIPTURE FOR THE DAY AND HOW IT WILL HELP YOU AS YOU MOVE TOWARDS YOUR PURPOSE.

Ephesians 2:4, I John 4:10

_____
_____
_____
_____
_____
_____

TUESDAY

STUDY THE CHAPTER ON THE WORDS <u>WONDERFULLY MADE</u>, WRITE OUT YOUR THOUGHTS ON THE SCRIPTURE FOR THE DAY AND HOW IT WILL HELP YOU AS YOU MOVE TOWARDS YOUR PURPOSE.

Psalms 139:14

WEDNESDAY

STUDY THE CHAPTER ON THE WORD <u>HIGHLY FAVOURED</u>, WRITE OUT YOUR THOUGHTS ON THE SCRIPTURE FOR THE DAY AND HOW IT WILL HELP YOU AS YOU MOVE TOWARDS YOUR PURPOSE.

Luke 1:28

THURSDAY

STUDY THE CHAPTER ON THE WORD <u>SPECIAL</u>, WRITE OUT YOUR THOUGHTS ON THE SCRIPTURE FOR THE DAY AND HOW IT WILL HELP YOU AS YOU MOVE TOWARDS YOUR PURPOSE.

Deuteronomy 7:6

_____
_____
_____
_____
_____

FRIDAY

STUDY THE CHAPTER ON THE WORD <u>LOVELY</u>, WRITE OUT YOUR THOUGHTS ON THE SCRIPTURE FOR THE DAY AND HOW IT WILL HELP YOU AS YOU MOVE TOWARDS YOUR PURPOSE.

Philippians 4:8

_____
_____
_____
_____
_____

SATURDAY

STUDY THE CHAPTER ON THE WORD <u>LOVELY</u>, WRITE OUT YOUR THOUGHTS ON THE SCRIPTURE FOR THE DAY AND HOW IT WILL HELP YOU AS YOU MOVE TOWARDS YOUR PURPOSE.

2 Samuel 1:23

SUNDAY

STUDY THE CHAPTER ON THE WORD <u>CONFIDENCE</u> UR THOUGHTS ON THE SCRIPTURE FOR THE DAY AND HOW IT WILL HELP YOU AS YOU MOVE TOWARDS YOUR PURPOSE.

Proverbs 3:26, Proverbs 118:8

LIST 10 WORDS THAT DESCRIBE WHO YOU ARE.

1.
2.
3.
4.
5.
6.
7.
8.
9.
10.

NOW TAKE EACH WORD FROM THE LIST AND ELABORATE ON EACH ONE OF THEM.

_____
_____
_____
_____
_____
_____
_____
_____

_____

_____

_____

_____

_____

LIST 10 SPECIAL WORDS THAT GOD SAYS YOU ARE FROM THE BIBLE AND ELABORATE ON THEM.

1.
2.
3.
4.
5.
6.
7.
8.
9.
10.

_____

_____

_____

***Purchase the Workbook for further study on this chapter*

13

Can These Dry Bones Resurrect and Live?

Faith Session 3

Can These Dry Bones Resurrect and Live?

Have you ever felt like you were in a valley of dry bones—a place where nothing seems to be working out, a life that seems dead, so dead that it stinks? Nothing seems to be getting better? Your life seems dry, dull, and full of gloom? This is what this chapter will talk about. It will show you how to make your dry bones live again. It will show you that God is your way out. He will make your dry bones come alive and live again.

There are times in our lives when being a Christian gets very dull and in your mind you're thinking, "Ok, what's next?", "I can't do this anymore, I give up!" "What have You sent me to this world to do Lord, sit and do nothing?" These are the words of those who have lost hope. Your circumstances have out weighed what the word of God has told you about God being a promise keeper. *[Hebrews 6:13-18]* God's promise—His oath is unchanging. It may seem as if God has forgotten about you and about the dream He has once shown you, but He hasn't. Many times we as Christians get anxious and impatient and the devil uses the spirit of fear, depression, oppression, and try to discourage you to believe that God will not do what He has promised. But I'm here to tell you that He will. I know you're waiting for me to talk about what God was saying to Ezekiel concerning the vision of the dry bones, but I want to let you know that God will never start something and not finish it. *[Isaiah 14: 24-27]* In Ezekiel chapter 37 God took Ezekiel to this place of dead dry bones and in verse 3, He asked him could these dry bones live? I believe what God was asking here was, can your situation change? Can you come out of the dry state that you are in? Can your finances get any better than just making it from pay check to pay check? Well, if you read the next verse, here is your faith answer. God is giving you your answer on how to make your situation change. In verse 4 God says: *"prophesy and say, "O' you dry bones, hear the word of the Lord. Verse 5, thus says the Lord God to these bones: Behold, (take a look at, watch, observe) I will cause breath and spirit to enter you, and you shall live."* You have to take hold of your life and command your situation to change by speaking words of faith and using the word of the Lord. Speak to those dry, dead bones in your life and tell them to change, tell them to live, tell your blessings to come to you right now. You must rebuke the devil and his tactics to make you quit and abort the promise that God is leading you to, and command your future to be blessed. Does this make sense? I hope so. In verse 7, Ezekiel did just what God told him to do, and as you read on it gets real good, Ezekiel spoke to the dry bones, there was a noise, a shaking, and the bones came together—bone to its bone. Then in verse 8, the sinews and the flesh came over them and covered them but there was one thing left out, there was no breath in them. Sometimes God will tell you to do something that doesn't make sense, but you know it's the right thing to do but you cannot see the total outcome. Another example is that you have obeyed God and it feels as if your breakthrough is right before your eyes and you cannot get to it. Just as God told Ezekiel to do all of those things to make those dry bones come alive, live, and look like something that wants to live again, but he had to do one more thing, he had to add breath in them. (in verse 10) Ezekiel obeyed God's every command and breath came into the bodies and they stood up and became an exceeding great army. God is saying to you: *"...even though your dry bones have lost hope and it seems as if the whole world is against you and have given up on you, but I will open your dead situation and cause you to come up out of your dead situation and bring you into a place in Me—a new land—a new level of life, love, and liberty. I will put my spirit in you, and you shall live, and you shall know that I am God. I the Lord have spoken it and have performed it, said the Lord."* That's great news! God has performed it already for you through faith, all you have to do is get up and get your life back and live again! You've been doing the same ol' things the same ol' way, going to the same ol' places, worshiping the same ol' way when you get in the mist of church service, following the same ol' people that mean your future no good, you've been doubting yourself and allowing the same ol' people to dictate your life. Trying to please everybody and they're still not satisfied. The Holy Spirit is telling you today that God is ready for you to go to another level. I believe this is in the mist of Ezekiel's purpose and I also believe that as God is showing Ezekiel the vision, He's also taking him to another level of faith in Him. God has to put you in an uncomfortable situation so that you will trust, lean, rely, depend, and totally obey Him during this time of transition and what seems like a dead situation; which is really a test of your faith. Can your dry bones resurrect and live? I believe they can, you believe and they will.

*I will put my spirit in you, and you shall live,
and you shall know that I am God.*

7 DAY SERIES OF STUDY
"CAN THESE DRY BONES RESERRECT AND LIVE?"

Name of Study:
Today's Date:
Focusing Scriptures:

7-DAY FAST 6AM-6PM

Eat only fruits and drink only water. You may eat soup no meats after 6pm. You will study and stand on the scriptures below by reading and confessing them daily.

MONDAY

STUDY THE CHAPTER ON THE WORD <u>RESTORE</u>, WRITE OUT YOUR THOUGHTS ON THE SCRIPTURE FOR THE DAY AND HOW IT WILL HELP YOU AS YOU MOVE TOWARDS YOUR PURPOSE.

Psalm 51:12

TUESDAY

STUDY THE CHAPTER ON THE WORD <u>RECONCILIATION</u>, WRITE OUT YOUR THOUGHTS ON THE SCRIPTURE FOR THE DAY AND HOW IT WILL HELP YOU AS YOU MOVE TOWARDS YOUR PURPOSE.

II Corinthians 5:18

WEDNESDAY

STUDY THE CHAPTER ON THE WORD <u>REVIVE</u>, WRITE OUT YOUR THOUGHTS ON THE SCRIPTURE FOR THE DAY AND HOW IT WILL HELP YOU AS YOU MOVE TOWARDS YOUR PURPOSE.

Psalms 138:7

THURSDAY

STUDY THE CHAPTER ON THE WORD <u>RENEW</u>, WRITE OUT YOUR THOUGHTS ON THE SCRIPTURE FOR THE DAY AND HOW IT WILL HELP YOU AS YOU MOVE TOWARDS YOUR PURPOSE.

Isaiah 40:31, Psalms 51:10

_____
_____
_____
_____
_____

FRIDAY

STUDY THE CHAPTER ON THE WORD <u>STRENGTH</u>, WRITE OUT YOUR THOUGHTS ON THE SCRIPTURE FOR THE DAY AND HOW IT WILL HELP YOU AS YOU MOVE TOWARDS YOUR PURPOSE.

Psalms 27:1

_____
_____
_____
_____
_____
_____

SATURDAY

STUDY THE CHAPTER ON THE WORD **HEAVINESS**, WRITE OUT YOUR THOUGHTS ON THE SCRIPTURE FOR THE DAY AND HOW IT WILL HELP YOU AS YOU MOVE TOWARDS YOUR PURPOSE.

Isaiah 61:3

SUNDAY

STUDY THE CHAPTER ON THE WORD **REJOICE**, WRITE OUT YOUR THOUGHTS ON THE SCRIPTURE FOR THE DAY AND HOW IT WILL HELP YOU AS YOU MOVE TOWARDS YOUR PURPOSE.

Philippians 4:4, John 4:36

LIST 10 AREAS IN YOUR LIFE THAT NEED TO BE RESTORED BACK TO GOD.

1.
2.
3.
4.
5.
6.
7.
8.
9.
10.

ELABORATE ON THE SCRIPTURE, EZEKIEL 11-14.

_____
_____
_____
_____
_____
_____
_____
_____

_____

_____

_____

_____

_____

FROM THE LIST OF 10 ABOVE, ADD SCRIPTURES TO EACH ONE OF THEM AND BELIEVE GOD FOR A CHANGE IN THOSE AREAS.

1.
2.
3.
4.
5.
6.
7.
8.
9.
10.

_____

_____

_____

***Purchase the Workbook for further study on this chapter*

14

When My Bones Became Flesh through Faith

When My Bones Became Flesh through Faith

I could not complete the chapter on, "Can These Dry Bones Resurrect and Live?" without expounding on another chapter concerning the dry bones called, "When My Bones Became Flesh through faith". I explained in the chapter, "Can These Dry Bones Resurrect and Live?" that you have the power and the faith to change a dead situation that seems as if it is impossible to change. You have the power to move old, depressing, unimportant things out of your life by simply telling them to move. You are what you speak. There is power in your words. I am a strong believer that you can do anything you set your mind to do. Is this correct? Yes it is. If you are hungry, you can go to the refrigerator, get some food out, and prepare it and eat it. If you want to listen to music, you go to your radio, turn it on, and listen to some music. If you want to hang out with friends, you get in your vehicle, walk, or ride the bus and go hang out with your friends. If you want to pick a fight or an argument, you start complaining and think of something negative with the person you want to pick the fight or argument with, and that will initially start a fight or argument. I have found that a person can do what ever they want to do whether negative or positive. I say that to say this, you can speak to your current, dead situation and change it right away. In this same chapter of Ezekiel 37, verse 6 says, *"And I will lay sinews upon you, and will bring up flesh upon you, and cover you with skin, and put breath in you, and ye shall live; and ye shall know that I [am] the LORD."* I believe this is when you have given up hope in yourself, your dreams, your vision, your life, your ministry, or your purpose and literally have said that you do not care anymore. Your life is over. Everything that God has promised you will not come to past. People are talking bad about you. You're being laughed at and ridiculed because of your current situation. But in this chapter it proves that your dry bones can come back alive and live. You can get everything that has been stolen from you back. I have said this all through this book. I am a strong believer that God will never start something and not finish it. You can give up and not finish it, but God will never give up. In fact, when God has chosen you to do something; He will not let you give you up. He will press at you, He will convict you, He will send someone to encourage you and tell you not to give up and that God has not forgotten about you. He has not forgotten about your labor of love, and how you have helped people, and how faithful you have been. Just know that your labor and love is not in vain. *[Hebrews 6:10, I Corinthians 15:58, I Thessalonians 1:3]* He remembers all of those times when you gave to help someone secretly and nobody knew about it. You didn't blast it to the world. God has not forgotten how you've been a good mother or father, done the best that you could do to raise your children the right way. No, He has not forgotten about you.

In that particular verse God is speaking directly to the dry bones. God is speaking directly to you. He is telling you that He will rebuild you all over again. He will restore you. He will bring you back from out of your sin or your dead situation where you have totally given up and make you a new person. *[2 Corinthians 5:17] "Old things are past away, behold all things have become new."* God can make you new. He can make your flesh new. You won't act, think, or look the same when God resurrects you, brings new flesh upon you, and give you a new life of freedom in Him. Do you believe this? I sure hope so.

I can recall a time, years ago, when I did not have a job and had given up. Every job that I applied to or interview with, either I was under qualified, or I was over qualified. I could not understand it. I was in a rage because while this was happening to me, I still had bills due and the bill collectors weren't saying that's ok don't pay us until you get a job. They wanted their money and by the tone of most of them, as you know, they wanted their money right then. I couldn't understand what God was doing to me and what He was allowing to happen against me. So I fell into a state of depression, did not want to talk to anybody, did not want to go to church and be around anybody; especially the ones telling me that God loves me and that I'm going to be alright. I also had to face those church folks that are strictly sent to the church by the devil to make Christians lives a living hell. They're hateful, nosey, full of mess, and just want to crucify you, and destroy your future. I had those who loved seeing me broke, who loved seeing me without transportation, who loved seeing me unemployed, and who loved seeing me go through. They loved crucifying me. But when I got tired of being sick and tired, I got up and spoke to my current dead situation. I told the spirit of depression to leave me at once. I started being positive instead of walking around with my head down and defeated. I earnestly sought God and He revealed to me what He wanted me to do. Notice I said that I earnestly sought God? See at first I was not really seeking God like I should have been. Instead I was too busy complaining and being negative. I had no faith. My bones were completely dry and the chances of them coming alive were zero. You have to literally tell yourself that you can make it and speak God's word like, "I can do all things through Christ who strengthens me" *[Philippians 4:13]* "...God's word will not return back to me void..." *[Isaiah 55:11]* "...I am fearfully and wonderfully made." *[Psalms 139:14]*, "I am blessed." *[Genesis 30:13]*, Deuteronomy 28:1-14], "I am more than a conqueror through him that loves me." *[Romans 8:37]*, "...God will keep His promise..." *[Romans 4:20]* As I began reading God's word and praying, things began to turn around for me. I finally got a job with benefits. I was happy. I got my life back. My bones became flesh through faith. It was like my life came alive again. It's nothing more refreshing when you can get your life and hope back again, especially when you've lost it. You may have lost your hope through the loss of a job, a divorce, an abusive marriage or relationship, God will give you your hope back just grab a hold of His deliverance and love. It's right there.

This chapter is so powerful God uses Ezekiel to do the impossible. He uses Ezekiel to resurrect bones that looked to be dead and will not be brought back to life. God shows His miraculous power through *[Ezekiel in 37:6-10]* by first putting flesh on the bones—covering them with skin, then by adding breath to them so that they can live. But notice the words in verse 10. It says, "*...they lived, and stood up upon their feet, <u>an exceeding great army</u>.*" This is powerful because this is how God will do you when you make up in your mind that you are not going to be defeated, get back up on your feet, get your life back, get back on your knees, get back in church, and start believing God again. You will become <u>an exceeding great army</u> just like those dry bones became when you allow your bones to become flesh through faith again. Do you believe that? I sure hope so.

I had no faith. My bones were completely dry and the chances of them coming alive were zero. You have to literally tell yourself that you can make it and speak God's word...

---

7 DAY SERIES OF STUDY
"WHEN MY BONES BECAME FLESH THROUGH FAITH"

Name of Study:
Today's Date:
Focusing Scriptures:

7-DAY FAST 6AM-6PM

Eat only fruits and drink only water. You may eat soup no meats after 6pm. You will study and stand on the scriptures below by reading and confessing them daily.

MONDAY

STUDY THE CHAPTER ON THE WORD <u>DRY LAND</u>, WRITE OUT YOUR THOUGHTS ON THE SCRIPTURE FOR THE DAY AND HOW IT WILL HELP YOU AS YOU MOVE TOWARDS YOUR PURPOSE.

Psalm 66:6

_____
_____
_____
_____
_____
_____

TUESDAY

STUDY THE CHAPTER ON THE WORD <u>DRY BONES</u>, WRITE OUT YOUR THOUGHTS ON THE SCRIPTURE FOR THE DAY AND HOW IT WILL HELP YOU AS YOU MOVE TOWARDS YOUR PURPOSE.

Ezekiel 37:4, Psalms 133:1

WEDNESDAY

STUDY THE CHAPTER ON THE WORD <u>LIVE</u>, WRITE OUT YOUR THOUGHTS ON THE SCRIPTURE FOR THE DAY AND HOW IT WILL HELP YOU AS YOU MOVE TOWARDS YOUR PURPOSE.

Ezekiel 18:21

THURSDAY

STUDY THE CHAPTER ON THE WORD <u>HOPE</u>, WRITE OUT YOUR THOUGHTS ON THE SCRIPTURE FOR THE DAY AND HOW IT WILL HELP YOU AS YOU MOVE TOWARDS YOUR PURPOSE.

Psalms 39:7

_____
_____
_____
_____
_____
_____

FRIDAY

STUDY THE CHAPTER ON THE WORD <u>POWER</u>, WRITE OUT YOUR THOUGHTS ON THE SCRIPTURE FOR THE DAY AND HOW IT WILL HELP YOU AS YOU MOVE TOWARDS YOUR PURPOSE.

Nahum 1:3

_____
_____
_____
_____
_____
_____

SATURDAY

STUDY THE CHAPTER ON THE WORD <u>PEACE</u>, WRITE OUT YOUR THOUGHTS ON THE SCRIPTURE FOR THE DAY AND HOW IT WILL HELP YOU AS YOU MOVE TOWARDS YOUR PURPOSE.

Daniel 10:19

SUNDAY

STUDY THE CHAPTER ON THE WORD <u>PEACE</u>, WRITE OUT YOUR THOUGHTS ON THE SCRIPTURE FOR THE DAY AND HOW IT WILL HELP YOU AS YOU MOVE TOWARDS YOUR PURPOSE.

Galatians 5:22

LIST 10 AREAS IN YOUR LIFE WHERE YOU STRUGGLE WITH HAVING PEACE.

1.
2.
3.
4.
5.
6.
7.
8.
9.
10.

WRITE A TIME IN YOUR LIFE WHERE YOUR PEACE WAS TESTED AND HOW YOU HANDLED IT.

_____
_____
_____
_____
_____
_____
_____

LIST 10 MOMENTS WHEN YOU WANTED TO GIVE UP BUT DID NOT. AFTER YOU NAME THEM, WRITE A SCRIPTURE FROM THE BIBLE NEXT TO YOUR LIST WHERE YOU PLAN TO USE AS A GUIDE TO HELP YOU GET STRONGER IN THOSE AREAS. YOU MAY USE THE EXTRA NOTES BELOW FOR EXTRA ROOM.

1.
2.
3.
4.
5.
6.
7.
8.
9.
10.

LOOK AT DEUTERONOMY 28:1-14. RE-WRITE THOSE VERSES ON A BLANK SHEET OF PAPER AND PUT YOUR NAME IN THE PLACE WHERE YOU SEE THE WORD "THOU". (YOU MUST USE THE KING JAMES VERSION IN ORDER TO SUCCESSFULLY DO THIS FAITH EXERCISE). TAKE THE VERSES THAT YOU JUST WROTE DOWN AND SPEAK IT DAILY UNTIL YOU FEEL BETTER, AND UNTIL

YOU FEEL YOUR DELIVERANCE AND ARE BACK CONFIDENT IN WHO YOU ARE IN KNOWING THAT YOUR FAITH, LOVE, AND LABOR IS NOT IN VAIN. YOU MAY HAVE TO USE AN EXTRA SHEET OF PAPER IF YOU NEED MORE SPACE.

_____
_____
_____
_____
_____
_____
_____
_____
_____
_____
_____
_____
_____
_____
_____
_____
_____
_____
_____
_____

***Purchase the Workbook for further study on this chapter*

15

Turn Your Water into Wine

Turn Your Water into Wine

Has God ever asked you to do something that seemed impossible, or did not make sense? There are times when God will tell you do something that looks crazy or impossible only to increase your faith and to show you that He is a miracle working God. The scripture that comes to my mind is *[John 2: 1-11]*. This came at a time when there was a wedding at Cana of Galilee and Jesus' mother was there—they were both invited. They all apparently had been feasting off of the wine and in verse 3, it says that it was gone. This was a perfect opportunity for Jesus to manifest God's miracle working power and for the people to see and to believe. Mary, Jesus' earthly mother, said that there was no more wine left. I ask myself the question of, "Why did Mary ask Jesus that question when there were other people there who could have simply went to get some more wine?" The answer came to me that Mary knew Jesus was special and chosen of God, and had the gift to do the impossible; and she believed that he would come with an answer and take care of the problem—and that he did. The bible says in verse 7 that Jesus told the servants, the ones that Mary instructed to listen to Jesus to fill the water pots with water. They filled the pots to the brim. My thought on this is that when God tells you to do something, do it to the best of your ability. The servants filled the water to the top because they knew that if Mary said to listen to Jesus, they were confident that everything was going to be alright; and they wanted to see how in the world was he going to turn that pot of water into wine. They couldn't visually see it manifested yet, but they were obedient because they knew that God wouldn't fail them. After they filled the water pots, the bible says that Jesus told them take some out and give it to the governor (the leader in charge) and as the governor tasted what he thought was water now wine, his faith was quickly increased. He didn't know where it came from all he knew was that the water that he tasted was now wine. He said it was good wine and thought they had kept back the best after the first batch of wine had ran out. Jesus used this miracle to manifest God's glory and also so that the disciples—God's people would believe in him.

There is nothing like the wine of Jesus. In sharing this powerful story of how Jesus performed this miracle as they, the servants obeyed, this is the way you have to trust God, fill your faith to the brim and do what God as told you to do even if it seems crazy or impossible. For example, if God has told you to move to another city that you've never been to or have never heard of before, do it, and do it over your ability. If God has told you to exercise and eat right, do it, and do it over your ability. If God has told you to go to a million dollar subdivision where the house of your dream is located, and tells you to go inside of the realtor's office and tell them that you want to buy the house you've been already praying for with no money to buy it, do it, and do it over your ability.

In this thing called **PURPOSE**, it's not always easy obeying the Lord and doing exactly what He tells you to do. There are times when you may have to be alone and you may have to cry sometimes. You may not be able to do the things your friends may do. It's all according to the anointing that God has placed on your life. I also believe there is somebody out there who wants to give up on what God has promised you. I can say with all confidence, understanding, and authority for you not to give up. Your blessing is right around the corner. All you have to do is **BELIEVE, OBEY, AND RECEIVE**. I came out with my first book that God had instructed me to do. I never knew that God would choose me to write books, let alone become a published author. My first book was published on faith. God gave me favor to fulfill His promise. The first book is entitled, "When Ramona Got Her Groove Back from God". After that book, I released my second book, which is entitled, "My Song of Solomon". After that book I released my third book along with my second book entitled, "My Song of Solomon Prayer Journal". Now I am releasing my forth and fifth book. I could not have possibly done this alone. I give God all the glory and honor that he deserves. God will tell you to do things that you never thought you would do in order that He will get the glory. He is in control and wants to show you all that is within you. Most of the time these are gifts and talents you never knew you had.

*God reminded me that I did do the right thing
and that He had not forgotten
His promise and that He will do what He said.*

Turn your water into wine means you're going to have to trust God to do the impossible, reach the unreachable, do the unthinkable, and see what has never been seen before. God will never tell you to do something that you cannot do. God will never put you on an assignment that you cannot complete—no matter how hard it is, or how difficult it may seem. Jesus turning that water into wine showed something in a way that no man could have gotten the glory. There was no possible way that an earthly human being could have turned that water into wine. If so, the people would have quickly given the glory to one of the people that was there. But He did it in such a way that only He could get the glory, and this is what God is doing in your life. He's taking you through these rough and uncomfortable moments in order to get you to the place in Him that He wants you to be. He's also setting you up for your blessings. God never sets you up for failure, but He always sets you up to win. Praise God, hallelujah! Thank you Jesus, that's good news! Do you believe that? I sure hope so.

*God never sets you up for failure,
but He will always set you up to win.*

7 DAY SERIES OF STUDY
"TURN YOUR WATER INTO WINE"

Name of Study:
Today's Date:
Focusing Scriptures:

7-DAY FAST 6AM-6PM

Eat only fruits and drink only water. You may eat soup no meats after 6pm. You will study and stand on the scriptures below by reading and confessing them daily.

MONDAY

STUDY THE CHAPTER ON THE WORDS <u>MIRACLES</u>, WRITE OUT YOUR THOUGHTS ON THE SCRIPTURE FOR THE DAY AND HOW IT WILL HELP YOU AS YOU MOVE TOWARDS YOUR PURPOSE.

Deuteronomy 11:3

TUESDAY

STUDY THE CHAPTER ON THE WORD <u>MIRACLES</u>, WRITE OUT YOUR THOUGHTS ON THE SCRIPTURE FOR THE DAY AND HOW IT WILL HELP YOU AS YOU MOVE TOWARDS YOUR PURPOSE.

Judges 6:13

WEDNESDAY

STUDY THE CHAPTER ON THE WORD <u>BELIEVE</u>, WRITE OUT YOUR THOUGHTS ON THE SCRIPTURE FOR THE DAY AND HOW IT WILL HELP YOU AS YOU MOVE TOWARDS YOUR PURPOSE.

Habakkuk 1:5

THURSDAY

STUDY THE CHAPTER ON THE WORD BELIEVE, WRITE OUT YOUR THOUGHTS ON THE SCRIPTURE FOR THE DAY AND HOW IT WILL HELP YOU AS YOU MOVE TOWARDS YOUR PURPOSE.

1 Thessalonians 4:14

_____
_____
_____
_____
_____
_____

FRIDAY

STUDY THE CHAPTER ON THE WORD TRUST, WRITE OUT YOUR THOUGHTS ON THE SCRIPTURE FOR THE DAY AND HOW IT WILL HELP YOU AS YOU MOVE TOWARDS YOUR PURPOSE.

Psalms 2:12

_____
_____
_____
_____
_____
_____

SATURDAY

STUDY THE CHAPTER ON THE WORDS MIGHTY ACTS, WRITE OUT YOUR THOUGHTS ON THE SCRIPTURE FOR THE DAY AND HOW IT WILL HELP YOU AS YOU MOVE TOWARDS YOUR PURPOSE.

Psalms 106:2

SUNDAY

STUDY THE CHAPTER ON THE WORDS MIGHTY ACTS, WRITE OUT YOUR THOUGHTS ON THE SCRIPTURE FOR THE DAY AND HOW IT WILL HELP YOU AS YOU MOVE TOWARDS YOUR PURPOSE.

Psalms 150:2

LIST 10 MIRACLES THAT GOD PERFORMED FOR YOU IN YOUR LIFE. THEY CAN BE SOMETHING AS SIMPLE AS, PAYING YOUR BILLS WHEN YOU DID NOT HAVE THE MONEY, OR SOMETHING MAJOR, SUCH AS, HEALING YOU FROM A DETRIMENTAL SICKNESS.

1.
2.
3.
4.
5.
6.
7.
8.
9.
10.

WRITE YOUR COMMITMENT ON ALL OF THESE MIRACLES.

_____
_____
_____
_____
_____

LIST YOUR THOUGHTS ON THE CHAPTER TURN YOUR WATER INTO WINE. USE THE NUMBERS AND SPACE BELOW TO DO SO.

1.
2.
3.
4.
5.
6.
7.
8.
9.
10.

***Purchase the Workbook for further study on this chapter*

16

When the Devil Steals Your Word of Faith

When the Devil Steals Your Word of Faith

> *Howbeit this kind goeth not out but by prayer and fasting*
> **Matthew 17:21**

One day, years ago, I was sitting and listening to a preacher preach his sermon. Just as I was sitting and listening to his sermon and the words that he spoke, they quickly went in one ear, and out of the other. In my heart, mind, and spirit, I wanted so badly to remember what he was preaching to the people and myself about. Don't get me wrong, his sermon were powerful and full of faith. But just as it went in one ear, the devil intercepted his words and made me forget them. This is what I mean when I say that the devil comes to steal your word of faith. The devil comes to steal because he doesn't want God's people blessed. *[John 10:10]* He doesn't want you to receive strength and knowledge because if you do, his power will be broken and you will be set free. *[John 8:36]*

I was encouraged and motivated to put my faith into action and do what the preacher said to do, but once I got home, the preacher's words of faith were as if I never heard them. I desired to do right but wrong was right there to steal what I had heard. Just as I'm talking about this, I'm reminded of a scripture in *[Romans 7:19-20]* where it talks about desiring to do good, but evil is always present. I desired to hear and to obey the words of the preacher but I allowed the devil to come in and open a door that brought this confusion in my life. That was a stronghold that I had to ask the Lord to break and He broke it. But He did not break it right away it took fasting, praying, believing, trusting, and HAVING A DESIRE to see my full manifestation and know that I could come out of the dry state that I was in. One day I was reading the word of God and the scripture came to me in *[Matthew 17:14-21]* where the disciples were questioning Jesus why could they not cast out an evil spirit that was in a boy who was demon possessed, and Jesus quickly answered by saying, *"this kind does not go out except by prayer and fasting" [verse 21]*. As I read this, I realized that this was the problem that I had. I was allowing the devil to steal my word of faith immediately after I heard it come from the preacher. So after further study on that scripture, God revealed to me that I was only praying against that spirit and <u>not</u> applying the word of God which was not enough. I needed some extra help in my warfare, so I obeyed the Lord and went on a fast and began to pray against the devil that was attacking me, applied the word of God as I prayed each day, rebuked that spirit by faith, and continued to do this during the fast. Before I knew it, that spirit had left. I believe that if you want to be delivered, God will immediately deliver you, but you must have faith that He can do it. Now don't get me wrong, sometimes deliverance is a process—it does not always happen over night. But I can rest-assure you that if you hang in there, keep applying the word of God, confessing that you are delivered by speaking in your healing with your mouth; and fasting, you will find that your deliverance will happen almost before you realize it. God moves according to your faith. I have found by being in ministry that when a pastor or a minister prays for, or prophesies too and for an individual, and if that prophesy or word of encouragement does not come to past, the person would blame the pastor or the minister. I have to tell you that it is not always their fault. Some of that is your fault because you have to have the faith that God can and will fulfill the prophesy or word that they spoke into your life. You cannot go by their faith, they're only obeying the Lord in giving you the word, but you have to have the faith and believe it for yourself, find a scripture and stand on it, petition God about it, and wait for Him to move. The bible says that faith comes by hearing, and hearing by the word of God. *[Romans 10:17]* You have to **BELIEVE FOR YOURSELF** that what they prophesied to you is a true word from God. But it must be a word from the Lord. God will never give a person a word that is not found in the bible. If you receive a word that is not from the bible it is a false prophesy. But a true prophet and word from God will always be backed up by the word of God—the bible and will confirm what you are going through. It will come to past.

...He did not break it right away it took fasting, praying, believing, trusting, and HAVING A DESIRE TO CHANGE to completely see my full deliverance and manifestation.

---

7 DAY SERIES OF STUDY
"WHEN THE DEVIL STEALS YOUR WORD OF FAITH"

Name of Study:
Today's Date:
Focusing Scriptures:

7-DAY FAST 6AM-6PM

Eat only fruits and drink only water. You may eat soup no meats after 6pm. You will study and stand on the scriptures below by reading and confessing them daily.

MONDAY

STUDY THE CHAPTER ON THE WORDS <u>STRONG HOLD</u>, WRITE OUT YOUR THOUGHTS ON THE SCRIPTURE FOR THE DAY AND HOW IT WILL HELP YOU AS YOU MOVE TOWARDS YOUR PURPOSE.

Nahum 1:7

TUESDAY

STUDY THE CHAPTER ON THE WORD <u>THOUGHT</u>, WRITE OUT YOUR THOUGHTS ON THE SCRIPTURE FOR THE DAY AND HOW IT WILL HELP YOU AS YOU MOVE TOWARDS YOUR PURPOSE.

Isaiah 14:24

WEDNESDAY

STUDY THE CHAPTER ON THE WORD <u>DELIVER</u>, WRITE OUT YOUR THOUGHTS ON THE SCRIPTURE FOR THE DAY AND HOW IT WILL HELP YOU AS YOU MOVE TOWARDS YOUR PURPOSE.

Psalms 119:154

THURSDAY

STUDY THE CHAPTER ON THE WORD <u>DELIVER</u>, WRITE OUT YOUR THOUGHTS ON THE SCRIPTURE FOR THE DAY AND HOW IT WILL HELP YOU AS YOU MOVE TOWARDS YOUR PURPOSE.

Psalms 143:9

_____
_____
_____
_____
_____

FRIDAY

STUDY THE CHAPTER ON THE WORD <u>PROTECTION</u>, WRITE OUT YOUR THOUGHTS ON THE SCRIPTURE FOR THE DAY AND HOW IT WILL HELP YOU AS YOU MOVE TOWARDS YOUR PURPOSE.

Deuteronomy 32:38

_____
_____
_____
_____
_____
_____

SATURDAY

STUDY THE CHAPTER ON THE WORDS <u>BIND AND LOOSE</u>, WRITE OUT YOUR THOUGHTS ON THE SCRIPTURE FOR THE DAY AND HOW IT WILL HELP YOU AS YOU MOVE TOWARDS YOUR PURPOSE.

Matthew 18:18

SUNDAY

STUDY THE CHAPTER ON THE WORD <u>OBEY</u>, WRITE OUT YOUR THOUGHTS ON THE SCRIPTURE FOR THE DAY AND HOW IT WILL HELP YOU AS YOU MOVE TOWARDS YOUR PURPOSE.

Colossians 2:20

LIST 10 THINGS FROM THE CHAPTER THAT HELPED YOU.

1.
2.
3.
4.
5.
6.
7.
8.
9.
10.

EXPOUND ON THE LIST YOU MADE ABOVE AND USE SCRIPTURE. WRITE ABOUT HOW YOU PLAN TO USE THIS IN YOUR LIFE.

_____
_____
_____
_____
_____
_____

_____
_____
_____
_____
_____
_____
_____

WRITE 10 SCRIPTURES CONCERNING, "RESISTING THE DEVIL" AND EXPOUND ON THEM ON THE LINES BELOW.

1.

2.

3.

4.

5.

6.

7.

8.

9.

10.

***Purchase the Workbook for further study on this chapter*

17

When the Lord Calls Your Name Say, "Here I Am."

When the Lord Calls Your Name Say, "Here I Am."

Then shalt thou call, and the LORD shall answer; thou shalt cry, and he shall say, Here I [am]. If thou take away from the midst of thee the yoke, the putting forth of the finger, and speaking vanity;

Isaiah 58:9

Here I am. Take the pain of my past away.
Here I am. I'm ready to do your will.
Here I am. I'm ready to fulfill my purpose.
Here I am. I'm ready for great success.

> *Calls you out of your past*

Has the Lord ever called your name? If so, did you answer Him? Did you believe that it was Him who called you, or did you think it was someone playing games with you? When God calls you, just answer Him by saying, "Here I Am". By saying this, this allows God to know that you are ready to do what ever He asks you to do. All God wants is a YES. So right now where ever you are, no matter what you are doing, who you are talking too, doesn't matter if you are laying down on the couch or laying across your bed, or on your job, or on the beach on a vacation, just tell God YES! He is waiting to give you instructions. Your purpose is caught up in your YES. Your assignment is caught up in your YES. Your YES will open the doors to the super natural—the harvest of breakthroughs. Not too many can experience the supernatural because at times it hurts too bad. When you tell God yes, He may require you to do some things that you do not want to do, and that hurts. But when you realize that if you just obey, He is required to take care of you and show you how to do what ever it is that He is asking you to do. I'm thinking about the times when God told me to do some things that I did not want to do, and the true fact that He would not make me do anything that was going to harm me. He was not going to make me do something that was going to put me to shame; He was not going to ask me to do something that He had not already answered in the supernatural. In faith, He has already answered what ever it is that He has asked you to do. So by the time you start doing it, it is already done because He has already answered it. Make sense? I sure hope so, amen. See, you have to start thinking in terms of faith at all times. When you talk to God you can't think in terms of the why not, why me, wo' it's me, no way, the I can't do it, or the how I'm gon' do it or get it done, you have to think in terms of the YES Lord, I'll do what ever You say and I thank You that it's already done by faith. If you are sick, don't ask Him to heal you, just thank Him with your mouth that you are already healed. If you're broke and do not have a dime in your pocket, do not ask Him for any money, just thank Him that you already have more than enough money in your pocket and watch the supernatural and the physical manifestation of His miraculous power operate for you. Glory to God, I feel a breakthrough in that word! Praise the Lord! I know you're receiving a breakthrough even right now! I'm reminded of Jesus, when He walked on the water and bid Peter to come out on the water and walk to Him. Peter was doing fine as long as his faith, focus, and belief were on Jesus. As soon as Peter took his eyes off of Jesus and the PURPOSE that Jesus had asked him to do, he began to sink; and to a point where he had to cry out for Jesus to help him. *[Matthew14:22-36]* This may be the same thing that is happening in your life. Jesus gave you an assignment to complete, you started it, and you were fine and you were seeing positive results and wam'! Something happened. Either somebody came against you, or you began to worry about petty things, you started doing or looking back at your past—old things you used to do, and you took your mind off of what God told you to do. Your focus was completely on the negative, which was the devil's plan, verses the positive, which was God's plan. If this has happened to you or is happening to you, don't give up, just repent by asking God to forgive you, go back to the "Here I am"—when you first heard His voice and start again. God will always keep His promise, and He will always keep His covenant with you, all He's waiting on is a YES!

He is waiting to give you instructions.
Your purpose is caught up in your YES.
Your assignment is caught up in your YES.
Your YES will open the doors to the super natural —
the harvest of breakthroughs.

God calls each one of us differently and at different times. You may recall if you are a bible scholar that God called Moses from the burning bush when He was calling Moses into His purpose. That purpose was to lead the Israelites out of the land of Egypt, into the land of Caanan—the land flowing with milk and honey. What I like most was the fact that Moses was imperfect. He had not too long ago murdered somebody. He would in this world be considered as a reject. But he wasn't a reject to God. God will sometimes take the foolish things to conform the wise. *[1 Corinthians 1:27]* God will sometimes take a person who by looking at their past and what they look like on the outside, change them, clean them up, and use them for His glory. You may be a Moses. Your past was messed up to a point that hell would be the only place left for you to go, BUT GOD forgave you, BUT GOD cleaned you up, and led you towards your purpose. Now you are telling others your testimony and what God has done. God will take a nobody—a person who knows they don't deserve the blessings that God has given to them, they're just grateful to be used and grateful to be saved; and God will use them to do more than those who think they're all of that, full of pride, got their noses stuck up in the air, a busy body, starting mess, who laugh at people who have an embarrassing pass, who think they are always right, who think they are never wrong and nobody can out do them; who think they are the greatest leader in the church, and a Moses can't possibly come in and take their place. God will take the foolish things to conform the wise…think about it, not too long, it'll make you sad. I am tired of this in this world and in the church. God has called each one of us to a certain purpose and you cannot judge each other because your past may not be as nasty or horrifying as others. God is no respect of persons *[Romans 2:11]* He will, can, and has changed billions from various types of lifestyles into a clean, liberated, and a restored life in Him. Praise God! This is what God did for Moses. Moses ended up being one of the greatest leaders in the bible. God never gives up on anybody. People may count you out and they may give up on you, but God will never give up on you. And that is good news! SO DON'T YOU EVER GIVE UP!

Calls you into the/your ministry

There's another powerful person in the bible that I'd like to use as one who God has called. Earlier I talked about Moses being called—someone who messed up and God still called him to do a great work. Now I want to talk about a young man who was called into the ministry at an early age, and his name was Samuel. Samuel was brought in this life by a praying mother who at first could not have any children. She was so deeply depressed about not being able to have any children. She wanted so badly to have a child but the bible says that the Lord shut up her womb. *[I Samuel 1:5]* She was highly favored and so loved by the Lord. You ever been there? You ever been in a place where you knew the Lord loved you but put you in a certain situation that you didn't feel you deserved? Well this was the position that Hannah was in. Look back at what I just said. I said that the Lord shut up Hannah's womb in verse 5. So you can plainly see that this was a work of God. This was the plan and purpose of God. It was obvious that God does things for a reason. He allowed this to happen to Hannah to draw her closer and to another level of prayer and trust in Him. If you are going through this, this is what the Lord is doing in your life. He's drawing you to another level in Him. God wants you to trust Him for everything you have. He wanted Hannah to trust Him no matter what it looked like. At the time it appeared, and notice I said, appeared. It appeared that Hannah would never have a child that she so longed for. But the bible says in verse 10 that she wept sore. Meaning that she cried until she couldn't cry anymore. She cried until the words wouldn't come out of her mouth. Ever been there? Ever been in a messed up place in your life and all you could do was cry until you fell asleep? You may be there right now. I've been there—many times in my life. But Hannah prayed, trusted, leaned, and relied on the Lord, and in verse 20 is when she received her breakthrough. She conceived a son whom she dedicated to the Lord. God kept His word. At first it seemed as if God was not going to bless her with a child but because Hannah did not give up, she prayed until something happened, she prayed until God moved and soon after, the child named Samuel was born. The bible says that Hannah gave him to the Lord, she gave him to Eli—the priest of the church at that time because she promised the Lord that she would give him to Him—God [verse 28]. At Samuel's early age he began to develop in his gifts. And one night the bible says that he heard a voice call his name three times and thought it was Eli calling him. So Eli told him when he hear the voice call him again to answer it. The bible says that Samuel did just that. When he answered the voice, it was God. God was calling him into his ministry—and that ministry was a prophetic ministry that changed many lives. I dissected this chapter in 1st Samuel because the only way you'll understand what you're going through, and how to come out of it, or how to change it, you must read the word of God—the bible. I can remember when the Lord was calling me into the ministry years ago. I didn't receive it at first because I was still doing things that I knew wasn't pleasing to Him. But He kept tugging and tugging at my heart until I answered. I can remember one day I heard a voice call my name and it wasn't anybody in the room with me. It startled me. It wasn't an evil voice, it was a soft, settled, and a very peaceful voice. It was a voice that was a voice of an angel's voice. The rest of that day I could not get that voice out of my mind. I was very confused as to why that voice would call my name. I did not think about being called to do anything for the Lord especially the fact that I was not perfect and didn't grow up in the church. The word, "gift" was the last thing on my mind. I wanted the truth about that voice. About a few weeks to some months later—can't quite remember but I was at a church that I attended at that time and the preacher that was ministering on that particular day was preaching on the subject of something like, "when God has a calling on your life, you need to except His call". When I heard those words, something ignited on the inside of me. I knew that subject was the answer to my prayers and it had everything to do with the voice that I had heard that other week or month ago. From there my life began to go up. God began to bring me up and out. I said YES to His will and He took those words and brought me to a place in Him that I had never been in before. So when the Lord calls your name, just surrender your will and answer Him by telling Him YES. I cannot say that my walk and my ministry has been perfect because it hasn't. There were times when I wanted to quit and give up. But somehow God always had a ram in the bush waiting to put me back on course again. Just like He's walking me up my ladder to my purpose, I believe He's walking you up your ladder as well. That is why He chose you to either purchase this book, or that is why someone gave you this book to read so that you can be healed and encouraged to get back on your ladder of purpose and follow God's plan for your life. The bible says that the race is not given to the swift, nor the battle to the strong..." *[Ecclesiastes 9:11]* But I believe that He'll give it to the one that endures to the end. You may be a Pastor or a Bishop that has gotten tired in your calling and is on the verge of giving up. I'm here to encourage you not to give up. Get back on your ladder of purpose, turn your faith towards your future, God will defend you and defeat the enemy who's against you. Every ministry gets hard at times. Life gets hard at times. Following what God wants even gets hard at times because God does not always tell you everything right away. He'll allow you to go through some things in order to make you stronger, in order to take you higher and put you in a place of total trust in Him. Make sense? Hope so. Hope you're encouraged.

God does not always call you like others think He should. You may be one that people have all of these expectations for you, your life, or your ministry; and they already have it planned out how you're going to come to the Lord and except your calling or how you're going to get saved and give God your life completely, but God calls everybody differently. You cannot worry about what people think, but just do what YOU feel that God is leading you to do. I know that He'll never lead you astray. People will, but God won't.

Calls you into your purpose

God designed each and every one of us to a purpose. This is the reason why you were created to come into this world. *"Created for honour, sanctified, (fit) meet for the Masters use, prepared unto every good work." [2 Timothy 2: 21].* God has already <u>prepared</u> you and He already knows what He wants to use you to do. It is never anything evil, it is always to make a positive difference and a life changing change in this world. The devil comes to make you think that you are no good and you'll never amount to anything. He sometimes uses those who are close to you to tell you negative things and to bring you down. But do not listen to them, you have been bought with a price, Jesus paid a price for you when He came down on this earth and died on the cross just for you. He PREPARED THE WAY FOR YOUR PURPOSE. Praise God! You have to know who you are in Christ. You are fearfully and wonderfully made. *[Psalms 139: 14]* You never have to give up thinking that God will never use you for anything, or your gifts and talents will never be used, or you're useless and nobody will accept you because of your past, or the illness you have will never allow you to fulfill God's purpose for your life, or you don't have any gifts so therefore your coming into this world was a waste of time. This is the devil speaking to you and you do not have to accept that. Remember what I said up top, you are fearfully and wonderfully made and you have the ability to do anything. *[Philippians 4:13]*

*God designed each and every one of us to a purpose.
This was the reason why you were created
to come in this world...
He has prepared the way for your purpose.*

7 DAY SERIES OF STUDY
"WHEN THE LORD CALLS YOUR NAME SAY, 'HERE I AM'"

Name of Study:
Today's Date:
Focusing Scriptures:

7-DAY FAST 6AM-6PM

Eat only fruits and drink only water. You may eat soup no meats after 6pm. You will study and stand on the scriptures below by reading and confessing them daily.

MONDAY

STUDY THE CHAPTER ON THE WORDS <u>LISTEN</u>, WRITE OUT YOUR THOUGHTS ON THE SCRIPTURE FOR THE DAY AND HOW IT WILL HELP YOU AS YOU MOVE TOWARDS YOUR PURPOSE.

Isaiah 49:1

_____
_____
_____
_____
_____

TUESDAY

STUDY THE CHAPTER ON THE WORD <u>OBEY</u>, WRITE OUT YOUR THOUGHTS ON THE SCRIPTURE FOR THE DAY AND HOW IT WILL HELP YOU AS YOU MOVE TOWARDS YOUR PURPOSE.

Jeremiah 7:23

WEDNESDAY

STUDY THE CHAPTER ON THE WORD <u>MOVE</u>, WRITE OUT YOUR THOUGHTS ON THE SCRIPTURE FOR THE DAY AND HOW IT WILL HELP YOU AS YOU MOVE TOWARDS YOUR PURPOSE.

Judges 13:25, *for more reading on this verse start at verse 1*

THURSDAY

STUDY THE CHAPTER ON THE WORD <u>HEAR</u>, WRITE OUT YOUR THOUGHTS ON THE SCRIPTURE FOR THE DAY AND HOW IT WILL HELP YOU AS YOU MOVE TOWARDS YOUR PURPOSE.

Genesis 21:6, *for further study (Genesis 21:1-7)*

FRIDAY

STUDY THE CHAPTER ON THE WORD <u>KNOW</u>, WRITE OUT YOUR THOUGHTS ON THE SCRIPTURE FOR THE DAY AND HOW IT WILL HELP YOU AS YOU MOVE TOWARDS YOUR PURPOSE.

Joshua 23:14

SATURDAY

STUDY THE CHAPTER ON THE WORD <u>BELIEVE</u>, WRITE OUT YOUR THOUGHTS ON THE SCRIPTURE FOR THE DAY AND HOW IT WILL HELP YOU AS YOU MOVE TOWARDS YOUR PURPOSE.

Hebrews 11:6

SUNDAY

STUDY THE CHAPTER ON THE WORD <u>LISTEN</u>, WRITE OUT YOUR THOUGHTS ON THE SCRIPTURE FOR THE DAY AND HOW IT WILL HELP YOU AS YOU MOVE TOWARDS YOUR PURPOSE.

Jeremiah 6:17

LIST 10 THINGS FROM THE CHAPTER THAT CONVICTED YOU.

1.
2.
3.
4.
5.
6.
7.
8.
9.
10.

FIND A SCRIPTURE TO GO WITH THE 10 AREAS YOU JUST LISTED. MAKE SURE THEY WILL HELP REMOVE THOSE AREAS YOU NAMED COMPLETELY OUT OF YOUR LIFE.

_____
_____
_____
_____
_____
_____

_____

_____

_____

_____

_____

_____

_____

LIST 10 THINGS THAT ENCOURAGED YOU IN THE CHAPTER AND IN THE 7-DAY SERIES OF STUDY AND WRITE YOU'RE NOTES ON THEM.

1.

2.

3.

4.

5.

6.

7.

8.

9.

10.

***Purchase the Workbook for further study on this chapter*

18

You Shall Have What You Speak

Faith Session 4

You Shall Have What You Speak

We as humans have the hardest time keeping our mouth's closed. Have you ever tried to stay quiet for the entire day without saying anything at all? Almost impossible right? It's nothing wrong with talking, we just have to watch what we say. We have to watch what comes out of our mouths. God is pleased when good, positive, and wholesome things come out of our mouths. He is not pleased when we speak things that are contrary to His Word *(bible)*. He wants us to speak words that edify, build up, and not tear down; words that encourage and bring someone into a blessed place and not a cursed place. You should speak words of blessing, and not words of hatred. At times we all have fallen short of speaking words that we knew we should not have spoken, but we should repent and ask God to help us in those areas of weakness.

If God is convicting you in this area, you need to pay close attention to Him. You are what you speak. You shall have what you speak. So if you speak words of blessing on your life, that's what you'll have. If you speak words of negativity, that's what you'll have. If you speak words of sickness, that's what you'll have. If you speak words of faith, purpose, and God's promise, that's what you'll receive. You may say, "I've failed in all of these areas, what do I do? How do I take away these things that I have spoken against myself, my family, against others?" My words to you are that God is a forgiving God. He is not an unforgiving God. He is very merciful and kind. God loves you so much that He's waiting to forgive you and put you back in right standing with Him. He wants you to win and to fulfill your purpose. He does not want the devil to get the glory in your life. In *[I John 1:9]* All you have to do is confess your sin to God by repenting for allowing those words to come out of your mouth, ask Him to forgive you, and then ask Him to deliver you so that you will not speak in that way again. If you do this, you're on your way to a positive, blessed life. I'm a strong believer when you love and speak highly of others, bless others, and speak words that will bring people to Christ, your days will be filled with the victory over every situation and you'll be blessed.

Many times we are so hard on ourselves when we mess up. We actually think that God will never forgive us and still bless us. This is the devil's way to bring condemnation against you and make you feel sad, down, and depressed. The bible says, *"Therefore, there is now no condemnation for those who are in Christ Jesus..."* *[Romans 8:1]* God does not come to condemn you, He only comes that you'll be convicted of speaking things that you know is not right against others, and against what is in the word of God. He wants you to stop and be healed. God has reminded us that He is true to His promise and that He will not fail us. You can fail you, but God will not fail you. *[Joshua 23:14]* So that's why you have to watch what you speak. I realize it's hard, especially at times when the enemy is right in front of you running his or her mouth, or sending darts of confusion. But you must remember that you do not want to say something that you'll live to regret. In *[Psalms 34:13]* it says, *"keep your tongue from evil, and thy lips from speaking guile (deceit)."* You must not use your tongue for evil vain words but use your tongue for positive, uplifting, loving words.

The bible also says that life and death is in the power of the tongue. *[Proverbs 18:21]* By not watching what you speak you have the power to speak words that will literally kill your purpose or your assignment. The only way it won't happen is if you quickly repent, ask God to forgive you and heal you from that struggle so that you can reap full blessing, and complete your purpose or the assignment that God has for you to do. Make sense? I sure hope so. Amen, praise God.

If we say we are Christians and do not brittle our tongues, our religion is worthless. Look in *[James 1:26]* it says, *"if anyone considers himself religious and yet does not keep a tight rein on his tongue, he deceives himself and his religion is worthless."* We as Christians have to set the standard for those who are not saved and need to come into the knowledge of who Jesus Christ is. You cannot do this if you're talking and acting like the sinners are. You cannot even witness to them. They're not going to want to hear what you have to say. You have to be in a position where people can just look at you and say, "I know she's saved or I know he's saved". And certainly when you speak they'll say I know he knows Jesus because he's speaking nothing but loving, Christ-like words. I know I can make it now. These are things they'll say or think towards you. But you must brittle your tongue. You cannot curse out your boss, or speak lies, and yell at everybody, or have such a bad attitude that people don't want to talk to you or they're too scared of you and scared to be around you. This is not bridling your tongue. Remember God is always listening and watching you even when no one's around you. I can say for myself that this is one of the hardest areas to get under control especially when attacks are constantly coming at you in different kinds of directions. If this is your hardest area to get delivered in, just remember Jesus had all kinds of words and attacks come against him but he bridled his tongue. He did not speak evil back to them nor did he curse them out, or give them a piece of his mind. He simply spoke the truth which was the word of God. He told the truth in love. This is what you have to concentrate on, speaking the truth in love or just keep your mouth closed. I have learned in times past when I practiced this method, it worked and I was victorious, but there were also times in the past when I did not practice this method, I fail short and had to repent. People cannot argue with themselves. You have to make up in your mind that you're not going to give any place to the devil, and you will find that your attacker(s) will quickly get quiet and leave you alone. It takes prayer and believing God to change in this area.

Position Your Faith for Great Success

At first it's not easy, but as you continue to stay in prayer and keep practicing the method that I mentioned up top, you will get stronger and it will become easy and you'll begin to see your victory and experience the reward of conquering this area. Do you agree? I sure hope so. Praise God!

I am an educator and I have had the experience of teaching students on the elementary, middle school, high school, and on the college level. I must say that this is the hardest level for the youth and young adults to conquer as well. The peer pressure is much harder. It's harder because they have to deal with both sides. They have to deal with peers that are on their side who pushes them to tell attacker(s) off that told them off. They do not want to disappoint them so they fall and do what there so-called friends have pressured them to do. They tell their attacker off or go so far as to even fight them and make matters worse. Then on other side where their attacker is coming against them, they tell them off or try to fight them back. Either way they loose. You may be a youth or a young adult and are experiencing this area of trauma in your life. My advice to you by being a teacher and college professor; and having being their and watching this, make sure you pick your friends wisely. It is always good to pray and ask God to send you a friend(s). You can never go wrong by doing this. Friends do not ever encourage or entice friends to do negative or sinful things. They will never tell you to tell your attacker(s) off and give them the best fight you can give them. If you have someone in your life like this, this is not a friend.

You don't ever have to run your mouth and fight a person who's in your face trying to attack you. Know who you are in Christ. **YOU DO NOT HAVE TO FIGHT YOUR BATTLES.** Let God fight your battles. If you do this, you will never loose. The worse mistake that you can make is to take measures upon yourself and try to fight your own battles without God. When you speak something that is contrary to what the word of God says, you can expect a negative outcome. This is why it is very important to constantly speak uplifting words of love, peace, unity, power, joy, and praise. When you speak this way, you can rest assure that you will have a better life, positive surroundings, you will feel better inside, you will see a change in the people around you, and you will graduate and take your next step up your latter of purpose. This is how you position yourself to have great success in your life. Remember without God you can do nothing, but with God you can do anything but fail.

In *[Proverbs 15:4]* it says, *"The tongue that brings healing is a tree of life, but a deceitful tongue crushes the spirit."* You are healed by the words that you speak. People are healed by the words that you speak. The church is healed by the words that you speak. The city is healed by the words that you speak. The world is healed by the words that you speak. It's important that you speak words of healing, words that are loving, words that are wholesome, words that save and not kill. You have the power to change the entire world by the words you speak. Use those words and watch and see a huge, positive change in your life for the better. Get ready for a blessed, wholesome, victorious life of liberty in Jesus Christ!

If you speak words of faith, purpose, and God's promise, that's what you'll receive.

---

7 DAY SERIES OF STUDY
"YOU SHALL HAVE WHAT YOU SPEAK"

Name of Study:
Today's Date:
Focusing Scriptures:

7-DAY FAST 6AM-6PM

Eat only fruits and drink only water. You may eat soup no meats after 6pm. You will study and stand on the scriptures below by reading and confessing them daily.

MONDAY

STUDY THE CHAPTER ON THE WORDS <u>MOUTH</u>, WRITE OUT YOUR THOUGHTS ON THE SCRIPTURE FOR THE DAY AND HOW IT WILL HELP YOU AS YOU MOVE TOWARDS YOUR PURPOSE.

Joy 7:11

_____
_____
_____
_____
_____

TUESDAY

STUDY THE CHAPTER ON THE WORD <u>MOUTH</u>, WRITE OUT YOUR THOUGHTS ON THE SCRIPTURE FOR THE DAY AND HOW IT WILL HELP YOU AS YOU MOVE TOWARDS YOUR PURPOSE.

Psalms 49:3

WEDNESDAY

STUDY THE CHAPTER ON THE WORD <u>MOUTH</u>, WRITE OUT YOUR THOUGHTS ON THE SCRIPTURE FOR THE DAY AND HOW IT WILL HELP YOU AS YOU MOVE TOWARDS YOUR PURPOSE.

Psalms 71:8

THURSDAY

STUDY THE CHAPTER ON THE WORD <u>MOUTH</u>, WRITE OUT YOUR THOUGHTS ON THE SCRIPTURE FOR THE DAY AND HOW IT WILL HELP YOU AS YOU MOVE TOWARDS YOUR PURPOSE. GOD HAS GIVEN YOU POWER.

Psalms 71:15

FRIDAY

STUDY THE CHAPTER ON THE WORD <u>SPEAK</u>, WRITE OUT YOUR THOUGHTS ON THE SCRIPTURE FOR THE DAY AND HOW IT WILL HELP YOU AS YOU MOVE TOWARDS YOUR PURPOSE.

Psalms 119:172

SATURDAY

STUDY THE CHAPTER ON THE WORD SPEAK, WRITE OUT YOUR THOUGHTS ON THE SCRIPTURE FOR THE DAY AND HOW IT WILL HELP YOU AS YOU MOVE TOWARDS YOUR PURPOSE.

Ezekiel 12:25

SUNDAY

STUDY THE CHAPTER ON THE WORD SPEAK, WRITE OUT YOUR THOUGHTS ON THE SCRIPTURE FOR THE DAY AND HOW IT WILL HELP YOU AS YOU MOVE TOWARDS YOUR PURPOSE.

2 Corinthians 12:6

LIST 10 THINGS FROM THE CHAPTER THAT YOU PLAN TO USE IN YOUR OWN LIFE.

1.
2.
3.
4.
5.
6.
7.
8.
9.
10.

ELABORATE ON THE 10 THINGS ON THE LINES BELOW.

_____

_____

_____

_____

_____

LIST 10 OF THE PROMISES THAT GOD HAS PROMISED YOU. ON THE LINES BELOW THE LIST, WRITE THEM OUT BACKING THEM UP WITH A SCRIPTURE.

1.

2.

3.

4.

5.

6.

7.

8.

9.

10.

***Purchase the Workbook for further study on this chapter*

19

The Foundation is Already Laid

The Foundation is Already Laid

Just

> **BELIEVE * OBEY * RECEIVE**

> **THIS IS YOUR SEASON OF OPPORTUNITY!**
>
> *YOU ARE ON YOUR WAY TO YOUR BLESSED, PROMISED FUTURE!*

Faith is the substance of things hoped for and the evidence of things not seen. *[Hebrews 11:1]* When you take the blindfolds off, you can visually see that the garden is already tilled—the foundation is already laid the way your purpose for your life is supposed to go. When you start thinking in terms of PURPOSE, you are moving towards your future, which is the promise that God has made to you.

The foundation is already laid for you to receive it. The key is, just receive it. Well, you may ask, "how do I go about receiving it?" Well the answer to that question is simple, **JUST RECEIVE IT**. All God requires from us is, **JUST A LITTLE FAITH**. The bible says in *[Matthew 17:20]* that faith the size of a mustard seed can MOVE MOUNTAINS. Do you know how huge mountains are? Moving one would seem impossible. But the bible says with just a little grain of a mustard seed can move a huge mountain out of your way. You may be experiencing some pain from your past, and you are having a hard time trusting God enough to deliver you and to help you to move on. Or you may be hesitant about trusting God to change your present situation around because in the past when you prayed for God to move, He didn't. Or you may have always paid your bills a certain way by just barely getting them paid, and you've believed God just enough not requiring anymore from Him to buy a little groceries for your family to eat. Or you may not have thought about having more for yourself at all. You may have said, "it just don't matter, as long as I have food to eat and my kids are taken care of." Well, I want you to know that's not all that God wants for you. God wants you to have more than just the average. <u>He wants you to experience the more than enough life.</u> Many times some Christians think it's just putting too much on God to have more than enough, and they're just satisfied with just getting their bills paid, along with all of the examples that I have just given to you above, but the bible says in: *[Deuteronomy 28:1-14, NIV]* beginning in verse 2 that *"...all these blessings will come upon you and accompany you if you obey the Lord your God: [3] You will be blessed in the city and blessed in the country. [4] The fruit of your womb will be blessed, and the crops of your land and the young of your livestock--the calves of your herds and the lambs of your flocks. [5] Your basket and your kneading trough will be blessed. [6] You will be blessed when you come in and blessed when you go out. [7] The Lord will grant that the enemies who rise up against you will be defeated before you. They will come at you from one direction but flee from you in seven. [8] The Lord will send a blessing on your barns and on everything you put your hand to. The Lord your God will bless you in the land he is giving you. [9] The Lord will establish you as his holy people, as he promised you on oath, if you keep the commands of the Lord your God and walk in his ways. [10] Then all the peoples on earth will see that you are called by the name of the Lord, and they will fear you. [11] The Lord will grant you abundant prosperity--in the fruit of your womb, the young of your livestock and the crops of your ground--in the land he swore to your forefathers to give you. [12] The Lord will open the heavens, the storehouse of his bounty, to send rain on your land in season and to bless all the work of your hands. You will lend to many nations but will borrow from none. [13] The Lord will make you the head, not the tail. If you pay attention to the commands of the Lord your God that I give you this day and carefully follow them, you will always be at the top, never at the bottom. [14] Do not turn aside from any of the commands I give you today, to the right or to the left, following other gods and serving them."* Do you see how blessed God wants you? All you have to do is, **JUST RECEIVE IT**. All you have to do is:

BELIEVE * OBEY * RECEIVE

God wants you to have more than just the average.

This comes at a time when God is laying the foundation for the earth and for His people. He's setting us up for His purpose of why He created the earth in the first place. It took Him 6 days to form the earth and on the 7th day he rested. But while He was resting, the bible says in *[Genesis 2: 5-6]* that God had not created any plants nor herbs and there was no one to **till the ground**. But before he created man to till the ground the bible says that He watered it with His mist or fog. I believe that this mist was His Holy Spirit which was the tilling of the land. This mist watered the ground to form all of the plants and trees—basically to form the Garden that He put Adam and Eve in to take care of. The name of the garden was the, "Garden of Eden". God laid the foundation because in verse 8 it says, *"...that the Lord made/planted a/the garden"*. Meaning He tilled the land which formulated the garden. All God created Adam to do was to take care of the ground. All Adam and Eve had to do was BELIEVE, OBEY, AND RECEIVE. All they had to do was to have faith that God had already laid the foundation by doing all of the hard work, and all they had to do was **receive the blessings that God had already laid before them**. All they had to do was REAP THE HARVEST. What I'm trying to say is, your blessings and promises are already set up all you have to do is, believe, obey, and receive. Many times we settle for less than what God has already stored up to give us. Did you know that there are hidden treasures on this earth just for God's people? *[Isaiah 45:3]* Do not settle for less. God is ready to give you what you deserve. You may be someone who has sown seed for years and has not seen your full due harvest from all of the seeds that you've sown. Don't settle by waiting any longer, get in prayer, take God at His word, and watch Him move for you. As I studied the topic that I wrote, "The Foundation is Already Laid, it has allowed me to understand how the earth was formed, why God created man and woman, how God had formed to earth for man to prosper. Powerful are the words that I can say, just powerful.

The bible says that they were on blessed ground. In Genesis 2: 10-14 it says that there were four rivers flowing through the Garden of Eden—this was a huge Garden. The first river was called Pison and it flowed through the Land of Havilah. And this land had gold in it. It was a very prosperous land. The land that God has for you is very prosperous. What and where is your land? Well, your land is the purpose that God has for you—it is located in your faith. And your land is also where the promise that God has promised you—it is also located in your faith. When you use your faith, apply the word of God, fast, and believe God, you will receive your land and all of the blessings that God has promised you. If He promised you that your body is healed, apply the word, fast, verbally confess, declare, and decree, and stand believing that

He <u>DID</u> do just what He said. I said the word <u>DID</u> because when you look/imagine it in the future tense, meaning before it happens, you will see and before you know it, your healing will have already happened and you will feel better before you even realize that God has already moved. Another example would be that the Electric Company has sent you a notice that your lights are going to be disconnected today if you do not pay the bill.

Before you call, you get your scriptures that say:

- *<u>Proverbs 3:5-6</u> Trust in the Lord with all your heart and lean not on your own understanding; [6] in all your ways acknowledge him, and he will make your paths straight.*

- *<u>Philippians 4:19</u> But my God shall supply all your need according to his riches in glory by Christ Jesus.*

You verbally say your confession of faith that says:

Lord I thank You for who You are. I thank you that I have more than enough. I declare and decree that in Luke 6:38 that man gives unto my bossom, pressed down, shaken together, and running over. I decree that I walk in faith and not in sight. I decree that I shall have what I speak. I declare and decree that my bills are paid owing no man. I thank You that there is no lack in my finances and my house is blessed. I stand on your word and I thank you for favor and that this decision will be in my favor. Amen.

> **Now you stand believing right before you call the Electric Company.**

The representative quickly comes on the phone ready to fulfill your request. You've already said your scriptures in faith, verbally said your confession, and believed that God will keep His promise through His word by supplying the need of the lights. As you are talking with the representative on the phone, you tell her your situation and that you do not have the money to pay your bill to keep your lights from getting cut off and she quickly says that they do not show that your lights are to be disconnected and that your account balance is zero. She also says that no one called and paid your balance either. You thank her and can't wait to hang up the phone and scream because God kept His promise as you stood on His word. This is the kind of faith that I am talking about.

The foundation is already laid, all you have to do is trust God, have mustard seed faith, stand on His word, and watch Him move <u>immediately</u>—before you finish praying. A great example I can use in the bible in reference to the word immediately is in *[Genesis 24:1-16]* where Abraham instructed the eldest servant to go and find a wife for his son Isaac. The servant set out to obey Abraham, and in verse 12 it says that the servant was praying to the Lord, asking Him to give Abraham favor with doing it fast *[immediately]*, show him loving kindness; and it says in verse 15, that before the servant was done praying that Rebekah came out and said and did <u>all</u> that he had SPECIFICALLY ASKED of God that she would say and do. See God will answer you while you are yet praying. This is how fast He moves. He moves before you can even know that you need help, or before you know that your lights are going to be disconnected as I showed in the example earlier, or before you know that you are sick in your body….etc. God is way ahead of you and He knows the plans that He has for you, and they are an expected end, not a dead end. *[Jeremiah 29:11]* Another key is in verse 14 when he was specific in his prayers of what he wanted her to say and do, that would be the sign to show that God moved for him. This is the way you have to be, you have to be specific in your prayers. The servant was specific. He wanted God to move in those specific areas and God did just that. Again, yet while he was praying, God did it. This goes with the example I used in the paragraph above with the person needing God to move immediately. They were specific, they prayed, verbally said their confession, and made the call by faith and as you can see, God did it. I have had this encounter as well. God had given me favor with paying a bill. I can recall a time when I had no money and the Electric Company had threatened to turn my lights off on a certain day. I had no job, no money, and prayed and believed God and the Electric Company never turned off my lights. Boy that was faith. At the time I did not realize how much faith I had. I was in a much move situation. I needed God to move and was tired of going through. I was in a state of depression and my house was a wreck. I didn't want to go outside. I had given up. I really needed God to do what He said that He would do in His bible. I'm sure this is what you are saying. You're saying, "I give up, at this point I'll try anything, I am so tired of going through, I can't take this anymore, I'm tired of struggling, I'm so tired of being broke and not having any money to go out and enjoy myself, or I'm tired of my kids not having enough and me not being able to give them the best." If you are saying either all or at least one of these statements, this would be a good thing for you to try. Actually this is the only thing that is good for you to try. God wants you to take Him at His word. He wants you to put your TOTAL trust in Him without wavering. I realize this is a very difficult thing to do especially if you are used to taking care of everything by yourself. When you take God at His word, He moves almost instantly or sometimes I have experienced Him just like the servant did.

He moved before I could finish my prayer. Without God's word—bible, we are nothing. Without God, we are nothing. You have to trust Him. I'm a strong believer that He won't let you down. Have you tried Him? Have you taken Him at His word and failed? Has He ever failed you when TOTALLY trusted Him to move? I can't think of a time when God failed me. I may have thought that He did, but He didn't. And he hasn't failed you. He's still more than able and ready to fulfill your every need. You just gotta' trust Him. You just gotta' BELIEVE, OBEY, and your outcome should be to RECEIVE. You believe this? I sure hope so.

God is way ahead of you, and He knows the plans that He has for you, and they are an expected end, not a dead end.

I know there are probably many of you saying, "how can I get to the point where I can have faith like that? I did not grow up knowing that I needed to have faith like this in order to know that God could move that fast for me. I was raised just to pray and not expect God to do the supernatural for me. I prayed like, if He didn't move it was alright or the lights just got cut off." If this is what you are saying, I want to help you. I'm not saying this as if I'm such a master at this, I'm still working on me in this area also. But I want to share this faith because this is what God is looking for in each and every one of us. He wants us to know that we are supposed to have more than enough. He wants us to know that we as His children are never supposed to be sitting in the dark with our lights cut off and not knowing when we're going to get the money to get them turned back on. God is faithful and His word is true. All He wants you to do is to trust Him and take Him at His word. And it says in His word that He promises to move *(help or be there for us)* and he cannot reverse it, nor can His word return back to Him void. *[Numbers 23:19-20]* This is the faith that we must have in order to experience the supernatural. If you are a youth who is in middle or high school, or you are a young adult or an adult who is a college student, you must have the faith to believe God to give you the brain, the memory, the mind, the dedication, the motivation, the desire, in order to past every test and to be an over achiever in every class or course.

Here is another form of the word foundation that I want to expound on. Even though God has already laid the foundation for you to be blessed, you must overcome some areas in your life that hinders you from being able to receive those blessings, and be able to walk in the faith that He has given to you through His word. God does not want you to follow the negative foundation of where you came from, He wants you to follow the foundation that He has laid through His word, and that is where your blessings and new life comes from. When you think in terms of the word foundation, you think of it as being the <u>base</u> or the ground work of something. Your life is <u>based</u> on the foundation of where you come from. How you were raised sets the foundation for your life. This is why you notice that you have the same traits as your parents or those who raised you. You may have heard someone say in times past that you act just like your mother or you act just like your daddy whether it is in a negative or positive way; or you may have seen or experienced a family member or a friend or maybe even yourself as being an alcoholic or drug addict and people have said that, they or you are just like your daddy or mother because they used to be on drugs or they used to drink and get drunk all the time or they still do. This is what I'm talking about when I explain the word, foundation. How you were raised or brought up is how you are going to act, the things you are going to do, how you are going to treat people, or the decisions you are going to make. If your mother or father suffers with depression, abuse, or a sex addiction, more than likely you or your siblings will too. This is the way the devil tries to destroy the generational blessings by turning them into generational curses. Here is another example of the word foundation. If your dad is a successful engineer, more than likely you or your other siblings will be also. If your mother likes to sew clothes, more than likely you or one of your siblings is going to like to sow clothes also. If your mother washed clothes a certain way, more than likely you or your other siblings are going to wash clothes the same way. If you were raised in an unclean environment, you are going to more than likely grow up doing the same thing. This is the foundation I am talking about whether it is negative or positive. You want to make sure that it lines up with the foundation that God's word says for your life. If those negative traits do not line up with the word of God, you should get in intensive prayer, go on a fast, and pray against those strongholds. All of the negative things that are passed down to you are the things that you have to pray against and seek God on how to remove them. Just because your grandmother or grandfather, or mother or father had cancer, diabetes, high blood pressure, or a severe illness, does not mean that you will get that illness. You can break the generational curse by praying against it, speaking against it; and by standing on God's word. Read and study the 7-Day Series of study and fast at the end of this chapter. Pray against those generational curses, strongholds, and soul ties for seven days. I believe that God will honor your prayer and fast and move for you. But it is in your faith. You cannot do this 7-Day Series of study and fast and speak negative against it and against the very things you believe God to remove and get miracle working results. God cannot move through unbelief nor can He move through doubt, nor can He move through hidden iniquity in your heart against Him because He hadn't moved in your life. You must rebuke those thoughts that will try to come in your mind and ears that will try to steer you astray from what you are believing God for concerning what you are praying for during the 7-Day Series of study and fast; and even what you are believing while studying, reading, and writing in your, "Position Your Faith for Great Success Workbook".

Remember, God's word is the foundation. It is already laid waiting on you to receive everything God has promised you to receive as you are climbing your ladder of purpose to success. The foundation does not always come in the form of money, it may also come in the form of emotional and physical deliverance and healing as I have stated up above. The generational curses, strongholds, and/or soul ties that you are carrying are not for you to carry. God has laid the foundation, which is the word of God, and you can be delivered from those things that have kept you from being able to receive your promised blessings. Amen? Do you receive it? I sure hope so.

The foundation does not always come in the form of money, it may also come in the form of emotional and physical deliverance.

---

7 DAY SERIES OF STUDY
"THE FOUNDATION IS ALREADY LAID"

Name of Study:
Today's Date:
Focusing Scriptures:

7-DAY FAST 6AM-6PM

Eat only fruits and drink only water. You may eat soup no meats after 6pm. You will study and stand on the scriptures below by reading and confessing them daily.

MONDAY

STUDY THE CHAPTER ON THE WORDS <u>CEDAR TREE</u>, WRITE OUT YOUR THOUGHTS ON THE SCRIPTURE FOR THE DAY AND HOW IT WILL HELP YOU AS YOU MOVE TOWARDS YOUR PURPOSE.

Psalm 92:12

_____
_____
_____
_____
_____

TUESDAY

STUDY THE CHAPTER ON THE WORD <u>UNITY</u>, WRITE OUT YOUR THOUGHTS ON THE SCRIPTURE FOR THE DAY AND HOW IT WILL HELP YOU AS YOU MOVE TOWARDS YOUR PURPOSE.

Psalms 133:1

_____
_____
_____
_____
_____
_____
_____

WEDNESDAY

STUDY THE CHAPTER ON THE WORD <u>LOVE</u>, WRITE OUT YOUR THOUGHTS ON THE SCRIPTURE FOR THE DAY AND HOW IT WILL HELP YOU AS YOU MOVE TOWARDS YOUR PURPOSE.

I John 3:18

_____
_____
_____
_____
_____
_____
_____

THURSDAY

STUDY THE CHAPTER ON THE WORD JOY, WRITE OUT YOUR THOUGHTS ON THE SCRIPTURE FOR THE DAY AND HOW IT WILL HELP YOU AS YOU MOVE TOWARDS YOUR PURPOSE.

Galatians 5:22, Philippians 1:4

_____
_____
_____
_____
_____

FRIDAY

STUDY THE CHAPTER ON THE WORD PEACE, WRITE OUT YOUR THOUGHTS ON THE SCRIPTURE FOR THE DAY AND HOW IT WILL HELP YOU AS YOU MOVE TOWARDS YOUR PURPOSE.

Isaiah 9:6

_____
_____
_____
_____
_____

SATURDAY

STUDY THE CHAPTER ON THE WORD <u>COMMUNICATE</u>, WRITE OUT YOUR THOUGHTS ON THE SCRIPTURE FOR THE DAY AND HOW IT WILL HELP YOU AS YOU MOVE TOWARDS YOUR PURPOSE.

I Titus 6:13, Hebrews 13:16

_____
_____
_____
_____
_____
_____
_____

SUNDAY

STUDY THE CHAPTER ON THE WORD <u>LISTEN</u>, WRITE OUT YOUR THOUGHTS ON THE SCRIPTURE FOR THE DAY AND HOW IT WILL HELP YOU AS YOU MOVE TOWARDS YOUR PURPOSE.

Isaiah 49:1, Psalms 143:1

_____
_____
_____
_____
_____
_____
_____

LIST 10 WAYS YOU'RE GOING TO STEP OUT ON FAITH.

1.
2.
3.
4.
5.
6.
7.
8.
9.
10.

NOW APPLY A SCRIPTURE TO THOSE 10 AREAS.

_____
_____
_____
_____
_____
_____
_____
_____

MAKE A LIST ON HOW YOU WILL WATCH YOUR WORDS YOU SPEAK TOWARDS YOUR PURPOSE, AND THEN ELABORATE ON THEM ON THE LINES BELOW.

1.
2.
3.
4.
5.
6.
7.
8.
9.
10.

***Purchase the Workbook for further study on this chapter

20

It's Your Appointed Season

It's Your Appointed Season

> *The word <u>Appointed</u> means: "chosen, selected, prearranged, to appoint"*
>
> *The word <u>Season</u> means: "period, time, term, time of year"*

What a perfect way to start this chapter by saying: "**THIS IS YOUR APPOINTED SEASON!**" Get ready for your blessings! You've gone through the storm and the rain, and you've made it. You've had so many up's and down's, and you're still standing. People said that you would never make it, but you've proven all of them wrong—you're still here, you're still standing, and you're headed to your land of plenty! This is why you can never give up! You can never give in to anything that is against what God has promised you. You can never settle for less than what God has told you, what He's going to give to you, or what He's going to do for you. *You must stay close to the vine* in order to fulfill your purpose and receive the promise. You must continue to climb your ladder of purpose. It may get hard sometimes, you may get tired, and you may even want to quit, but you can't you must continue to climb, this is your appointed season. There's no time to quit, you're too close. In *[Deuteronomy 15:1-5]* It talks about this being the year of release! Every creditor will have to release your debts. This is your year of plenty!

Climbing a ladder is not the easiest thing to do especially if you're not used to climbing. Well, it's the same thing as climbing the ladder to your success, and to your purpose, and to your destiny in life. When you start off climbing it's fairly easy because you're not using those excessive muscles yet, but as you continue to climb, those excessive muscles will begin to burn because they are being used. When God is pulling you up the ladder, many times He will allow you to get tired because He's building up your muscles of faith, meaning He's making you stronger so that you can continue to climb to reach your destiny, which is your purpose in life. I have found that if you allow God to make you stronger and go through those rough and tough times in your life and ministry, He will make it easier for you because you are showing Him that you trust Him and that you are not complaining while you're going up your ladder of success, purpose, and destiny.

This is your season to get back everything that the devil has stolen from you. I'm reminded about a powerful man named Jehoshaphat in *[II Chronicles 20:1-26]*. Jehoshaphat and all of Judah were in the process of being attacked by their enemies—the Moabites, the Ammonites, and the Meunites. In other words, their haters. They were of great multitudes. It was so many of them that they could not be counted. Anybody would be scared and would panic. But what I love about Jehoshaphat is the fact that he may have been afraid, but the bible says that he set himself to seek the Lord. *[verse 3]* This is what you have got to do when the devil comes up against you. You must not seek man first, but seek God first. When you seek God first, He'll show you what to do and what <u>not</u> to do. You must know that the devil is not going to roll over and die. He's going to try his tricks and schemes to try to stop you from receiving all that God has for you. You can quickly put the devil in his place by seeking God, fasting, applying the word of God, and getting with a trusted prayer partner of faith. Not only did Jehoshaphat set himself to seek the Lord, but he proclaimed a fast throughout all of Judah. He got the people involved. He knew that he couldn't fight nor protect himself all by himself. He needed help. This may be the same for you. Sometimes we as Christians grow weak and we need help with faith and with praying through until we get an answer. It's nothing wrong with teaming up with a prayer partner of faith. Notice I said <u>faith</u>. If that person is not talking faith, walking faith, or living faith, they have no faith and you're with the wrong faith partner. A prayer partner of faith is someone who's going to talk, walk, and live positive even when they cannot visually see your breakthrough, or how it's going to workout for you. They trust God for you and with you until they see God move in your circumstances.

They're going to always have the right attitude. You will never hear them talking negative or spreading your business to others, or saying God will never move for you.

What I love about the outcome of Jehoshaphat's trial was that he did all that God told him to do as the Lord GAVE INSTRUCTION. God gave specific instructions to Jehoshaphat and all of Judah through the prophet Jahaziel the son of Zechariah. The spirit of the Lord came upon him and said in *[verse 16-17]*, *"Be not afraid or dismayed at this great multitude; for the battle is not yours, but God's. [17] Ye shall not need to fight in this battle: set yourselves, stand still, and see the salvation of the Lord with you, O Judah and Jerusalem: fear not, nor be dismayed: tomorrow go out against them: for the Lord will be with you."* When God gives you a prophetic word like that, you can rest assure that it will come to past. God said that this is your appointed season and no matter what battles are up against you, no matter how many giants are up against you, God's word will prevail. He lets you know this in *verse [22]* that giants do fall. The bible says that their enemies began to come against each other and defeated each other. The enemy battled against themselves. Jehoshaphat and all of Judah never had to lift a finger; all they had to do was to give God the praise! And this is all you have to do is to give God the praise while your enemies defeat themselves in your appointed season. Now this is the grand finale. The bible says in verse *[25]* that there were so much stuff, so many blessings left from the defeated enemies that it took Jehoshaphat and all of Judah three whole days to gather all of the spoil. What is the spoil? The spoil is your abundance of blessings. Get ready to gather your abundance of finances, your new home, your new land, your new job, your new family! There shall be no more lack in your life. You may be someone in the gospel and the enemy is great up against you. Now is the time to seek God like never before. Proclaim a fast for yourself, stay faithful to the church that God has assigned you to, come together and pray with your faith partner or ministry group at your local church, and give God the praise until you see ambushments against the enemy in your life, home, family, career, and ministry. God will prevail just like He did for Jehoshaphat and all of Judah. God made a promise to bless them. God has made a promise to bless you so do not be afraid, lift a finger, raise your voice, or give up and throw in the towel. All you are instructed to do is to believe, give God praise, watch God make your enemies fight each other, and lastly, _gather_ the blessings for obeying God. This is your appointed season! Do you realize how many blessings God has for you to receive? There are so many that it's going to take more than a day for you to receive them all. You may be believing God for a new home and the land to build it on. You're discouraged because it seems as if all of your friends and everybody around you are getting their homes and all of the land; and for you it seems impossible to get blessed like them. You attempt to go to the bank but they will not budge towards your vision and towards your account. In fact, they have declined the fact that they are going to give you the loan because your credit is too bad and way too many delinquencies. But I want you to know that God will intercept your account and turn the verdict around on your behalf. God will perform everything that He has promised to you, but you must believe, obey, and receive. You cannot grow weary and tired. It's no time to quit and give up. You must be in it to win it. The race is not given to the weak, but it's given to the strong, which is the one who endures until the end. You must know that the pain is over. The drama in your life is over. The word hardship is defeated in your life. Get ready, get ready, get ready for your return! Get ready for your harvest! Amen? Amen! Praise God! Hallelujah that's good news!

If you studied Jehoshaphat's story in the beginning, you would probably wonder how in the world were they going to get out of that attack? This is what I love about God. God does not look at the outer appearance. He does not go by what it looks like visually, but He goes by what He has told you. He told Jehoshaphat and all of Judah that they need not have to fight, all they had to do is believe and give God the praise while He set ambushments against their enemies. God did just that and He gave all of them more than what they deserved in their appointed season. There is never a moment of defeat in your appointed season. You'll always be on top in your appointed season. Now where the hardship and the set back comes is when you stop moving up the ladder, become complacent, too comfortable, lazy, disobedient, lack showing your love, get off focus, and open the door to the devil in areas that would make you not seek God. This is when you give the devil the opportunity to steal your appointed season. I realize by reading this, if the shoe fits you, you can be very discouraged and immediately want to give up especially since you've already messed up and you feel as if you cannot get back what you've lost. NOT! It ain't over til' the lady sings.... God never gives up on you! He's still pulling for you. He has a promise to keep. *[II Corinthians 1:20]* All you have to do is repent, ask God to help you in those areas of weakness, and start climbing your ladder again. Watch God change things around in your life for the better. I believe it's still your season of opportunity! Amen? Praise God!

God said that this is your appointed season and no matter what battles are up against you, no matter how many giants are up against you, God's word will prevail.

---

7 DAY SERIES OF STUDY
"IT'S YOUR APPOINTED SEASON"

Name of Study:
Today's Date:
Focusing Scriptures:

7-DAY FAST 6AM-6PM

Eat only fruits and drink only water. You may eat soup no meats after 6pm. You will study and stand on the scriptures below by reading and confessing them daily.

MONDAY

STUDY THE CHAPTER ON THE WORDS <u>CEDAR TREE</u>, WRITE OUT YOUR THOUGHTS ON THE SCRIPTURE FOR THE DAY AND HOW IT WILL HELP YOU AS YOU MOVE TOWARDS YOUR PURPOSE.

Psalm 92:12

TUESDAY

STUDY THE CHAPTER ON THE WORD UNITY, WRITE OUT YOUR THOUGHTS ON THE SCRIPTURE FOR THE DAY AND HOW IT WILL HELP YOU AS YOU MOVE TOWARDS YOUR PURPOSE.

Psalms 133:1

_____
_____
_____
_____
_____
_____
_____

WEDNESDAY

STUDY THE CHAPTER ON THE WORD LOVE, WRITE OUT YOUR THOUGHTS ON THE SCRIPTURE FOR THE DAY AND HOW IT WILL HELP YOU AS YOU MOVE TOWARDS YOUR PURPOSE.

I John 3:18

_____
_____
_____
_____
_____
_____
_____

THURSDAY

STUDY THE CHAPTER ON THE WORD JOY, WRITE OUT YOUR THOUGHTS ON THE SCRIPTURE FOR THE DAY AND HOW IT WILL HELP YOU AS YOU MOVE TOWARDS YOUR PURPOSE.

Galatians 5:22, Philippians 1:4

_____
_____
_____
_____
_____

FRIDAY

STUDY THE CHAPTER ON THE WORD PEACE, WRITE OUT YOUR THOUGHTS ON THE SCRIPTURE FOR THE DAY AND HOW IT WILL HELP YOU AS YOU MOVE TOWARDS YOUR PURPOSE.

Isaiah 9:6

_____
_____
_____
_____
_____
_____

SATURDAY

STUDY THE CHAPTER ON THE WORD <u>COMMUNICATE</u>, WRITE OUT YOUR THOUGHTS ON THE SCRIPTURE FOR THE DAY AND HOW IT WILL HELP YOU AS YOU MOVE TOWARDS YOUR PURPOSE.

I Titus 6:13, Hebrews 13:16

SUNDAY

STUDY THE CHAPTER ON THE WORD <u>LISTEN</u>, WRITE OUT YOUR THOUGHTS ON THE SCRIPTURE FOR THE DAY AND HOW IT WILL HELP YOU AS YOU MOVE TOWARDS YOUR PURPOSE.

Isaiah 49:1, Psalms 143:1

LIST 10 WAYS YOU PLAN TO PREPARE FOR YOUR APPOINTED SEASON.

1.
2.
3.
4.
5.
6.
7.
8.
9.
10.

WRITE YOUR COMMITMENTS ON THE CHAPTER, "IT'S YOUR APPOINTED SEASON".

_____
_____
_____
_____
_____
_____
_____
_____

_____
_____
_____
_____
_____
_____

LIST 10 WAYS YOU ARE GOING TO CHANGE YOUR PRAYER LIFE TO PREPARE FOR YOUR APPOINTED SEASON. WRITE YOUR COMMENTS BELOW YOUR LIST.

1.
2.
3.
4.
5.
6.
7.
8.
9.
10.

***Purchase the Workbook for further study on this chapter*

21

Stay Close to the Vine

Stay Close to the Vine

It is important to know who the true vine is. The true vine is the Lord. If you break the vine, you break any contact you have with the Lord. There is no vine except it be the Lord. "I AM" is the vine. If you abide in the vine, you abide with, "I AM". This is why you can ask what you want and it will be done for you. This is also why you can do nothing without the Lord. But with the Lord, the true vine, you bear much fruit. Read and closely study the scripture I have written out for you. These scriptures explain what I am saying to you concerning why it is important to stay close to the vine. *[John 15:1-7]* "*<u>I AM the true vine</u>, and my Father is the husbandman. [2] Every branch in me that beareth not fruit he taketh away; and every branch that beareth fruit, he purgeth it, that it may bring forth more fruit. [3] Now ye are clean through the word which I have spoken unto you. [4] Abide in me, and I in you. As the branch cannot bear fruit of itself, except it abide in the vine; no more can ye, except ye abide in me. [5] I am the vine, ye are the branches: He that abideth in me, and I in him, the same bringeth forth much fruit; for without me ye can do nothing. [6] If a man abide not in me, he is cast forth as a branch, and is withered; and men gather them, and cast them into the fire, and they are burned. [7] If ye abide in me, and my words* *abide in you, ye shall ask what ye will, and it shall be done unto you."*

Staying close to the vine is how you're going to be able to turn your faith towards your future. You have no future unless you are close to the vine. I just explained who the vine is through my words and through the scriptures in the Holy Bible. God is the way and the life. He is your way—the only way, and your life—the only life. I'll explain a little more in my next paragraphs.

While it is your season you must stay close to the vine. You cannot waver nor can you doubt. You must keep your ears open to the voice of God, obey His voice, and move when He tells you to move. God only knows the exact moment He is ready to bless you and you must be in a position to receive. When you're not in position to receive, this means you are looking and listening to the wrong voice. The word of God says that, "my sheep hears my voice and I know them, and they follow me." *[John 10:27]* You cannot look to people in order to get a word from God. People only know so much. They are not God. People—Humans are not designed to know more than God if so, they would be God and therefore there would not be any reason to keep this world going because then we would all have the right answer, know everything, and not need God for anything. This is impossible. God did not create man to do his own thing, nor did He create man to be God. When God created the Heaven and the earth, He put man on it to till it and keep it looking nice. *[Genesis 2:5, 15]*

This was an instruction. You must listen to God and He will tell you what your purpose and destiny is. He will always guide you up and not down. God has special plans for you and He will never give up on you until your purpose is complete. The only flaw in this is that you are required to have faith in order for it to come to past. No faith, no purpose. No purpose, no story. No story, no God's glory. This is why people can die and not ever fulfill their purpose because they didn't believe God for it. They did not allow God to put them in position to complete it. And you may say, "well I disagree because the people that I know that have died were in the church and serving the Lord. Why did they die and not fulfill their purpose?" I'll have to answer this by saying that they did fulfill their purpose. They were saved, serving God, and allowing God to use them for the time that they had here on earth. We cannot predict or foretell our time to go home to be with the Lord. We have to stay looking up, keeping an open ear, obeying every word of the Lord, and climbing up our ladders of faith, purpose, and destiny. When you do this, this is how you position your faith for great success. Now all you have to do is walk in it.

It is important to know who the true vine is.
The true vine is the Lord.

---

*No faith, no purpose. No purpose, no story.
No story, no God's glory.*

7 DAY SERIES OF STUDY
"STAY CLOSE TO THE VINE"

Name of Study:
Today's Date:
Focusing Scriptures:

7-DAY FAST 6AM-6PM

Eat only fruits and drink only water. You may eat soup no meats after 6pm. You will study and stand on the scriptures below by reading and confessing them daily.

MONDAY

STUDY THE CHAPTER ON THE WORDS <u>CEDAR TREE</u>, WRITE OUT YOUR THOUGHTS ON THE SCRIPTURE FOR THE DAY AND HOW IT WILL HELP YOU AS YOU MOVE TOWARDS YOUR PURPOSE.

Psalm 92:12

_____
_____
_____
_____
_____

TUESDAY

STUDY THE CHAPTER ON THE WORD <u>UNITY</u>, WRITE OUT YOUR THOUGHTS ON THE SCRIPTURE FOR THE DAY AND HOW IT WILL HELP YOU AS YOU MOVE TOWARDS YOUR PURPOSE.

Psalms 133:1

WEDNESDAY

STUDY THE CHAPTER ON THE WORD <u>LOVE</u>, WRITE OUT YOUR THOUGHTS ON THE SCRIPTURE FOR THE DAY AND HOW IT WILL HELP YOU AS YOU MOVE TOWARDS YOUR PURPOSE.

I John 3:18

Position Your Faith for Great Success

THURSDAY

STUDY THE CHAPTER ON THE WORD <u>JOY</u>, WRITE OUT YOUR THOUGHTS ON THE SCRIPTURE FOR THE DAY AND HOW IT WILL HELP YOU AS YOU MOVE TOWARDS YOUR PURPOSE.

Galatians 5:22, Philippians 1:4

_____
_____
_____
_____
_____
_____

FRIDAY

STUDY THE CHAPTER ON THE WORD <u>PEACE</u>, WRITE OUT YOUR THOUGHTS ON THE SCRIPTURE FOR THE DAY AND HOW IT WILL HELP YOU AS YOU MOVE TOWARDS YOUR PURPOSE.

Isaiah 9:6

_____
_____
_____
_____
_____
_____

SATURDAY

STUDY THE CHAPTER ON THE WORD <u>COMMUNICATE</u>, WRITE OUT YOUR THOUGHTS ON THE SCRIPTURE FOR THE DAY AND HOW IT WILL HELP YOU AS YOU MOVE TOWARDS YOUR PURPOSE.

I Titus 6:13, Hebrews 13:16

SUNDAY

STUDY THE CHAPTER ON THE WORD <u>LISTEN</u>, WRITE OUT YOUR THOUGHTS ON THE SCRIPTURE FOR THE DAY AND HOW IT WILL HELP YOU AS YOU MOVE TOWARDS YOUR PURPOSE.

Isaiah 49:1, Psalms 143:1

LIST 10 SPECIAL THINGS ABOUT YOURSELF.

1.
2.
3.
4.
5.
6.
7.
8.
9.
10.

WRITE YOUR COMMITMENTS OVER THE CHAPTER.

_____
_____
_____
_____
_____
_____
_____
_____

WRITE 10 SCRIPTURES OVER THE CHAPTER AND HOW YOU ARE GOING TO APPLY THIS TO YOUR LIFE.

1.
2.
3.
4.
5.
6.
7.
8.
9.
10.

***Purchase the Workbook for further study on this chapter*

Scripture by Chapter Index

Note: All scriptures are from the KJV*Amplified Version in the Holy Bile.

***** FAITH SESSION 1 *****

CHAPTER 1:   *Birthing Your Pain from Your Purpose*

Isaiah 44:2, Jeremiah 1:5, Jeremiah 29:11, Ephesians 4:11-12, 1 Corinthians 12:3-10.

CHAPTER 2:   *Hell Faith to Heaven Faith*

Galatians 6:14, 1 Corinthians 10:31, John 10:10, Hebrews 11:6, Numbers 23:19-20

CHAPTER 3:   *Faith as Easy as Saying 1, 2, 3*

Genesis 14:13-19, 1 John 5:15, 1 Samuel 17, Ephesians 6:10-18, Genesis 37, 1 John 4:21

CHAPTER 4:   *Prosperity Come to me Right Now!*

Romans 8:17, Matthew 21:21, Matthew 21:21-22, Proverbs 3:6, Proverbs 13:22

CHAPTER 5: *Don't Panic, it's Only a Test*

Romans 5:1-4, Romans 4:20-21, Isaiah 53:5, 3 John 2, Genesis 18:17, Psalms 55:22, 1 Corinthians 10:13

CHAPTER 6: *It's a Set Up*

Romans 8:18, Ecclesiastes 3:1-15, Matthew 26: 36-42, Numbers 23:19-20, 2 Chronicles 20:15-18, Genesis 15, 16, 17, Romans 4:20-21, Philippians 4:19, Jeremiah 29:11

***** **FAITH SESSION 2** *****

CHAPTER 7: *Iron Sharpens Iron*

Malachi 3:2-3, Jeremiah 18:1-6, Ephesians 4:23, Isaiah 59:19, Proverbs 16:18, Proverbs 29:23, Romans 12:2, John 17:16, 1 John 2:15-17, 1 Peter 3:14, Deuteronomy 28:1-14, Romans 12:2, Deuteronomy 20:4, Isaiah 55:8, Matthew 5:48, Psalms 39:1, Psalms 37:27, Psalms 39:1, Psalms 37:27, James 4:7, Matthew 5:48, Psalms 51:2, 51:10

CHAPTER 8: *Two Heads Are Better Than One*

Ecclesiastes 4:9, John 10:10, 1 Thessalonians 5:17, 1 John 4:1

CHAPTER 9: *You Are Special Like the Cedar Tree*

Hebrews 13:8, Ezekiel 31:1-9, John 7:38, Matthew 5:6, Matthew 22:14, 1 John 2:1-2, Matthew 23:12, Psalms 68:1

CHAPTER 10: *Don't Judge A Book by its Cover*

2 Chronicles 29:35-36, Hebrews 13:1-2, Philippians 2:3

CHAPTER 11: *The Potter and the Clay*

Philippians 4:18

CHAPTER 12: *I'm All That God Say's I Am*

Deuteronomy 7:6, Deuteronomy 7:6, Jeremiah 29:11-13, Hebrews 13:5, John 11:11, 14, 43, Haggai 2:9, Philippians 2:3, 1 Thessalonians 5:13, Ephesians 5:27, Joshua 23:14

***** **FAITH SESSION 3** *****

CHAPTER 13: *Can these Dry Bones Resurrect and Live?*

Hebrews 6:13-18, Isaiah 14:24-27, Ezekiel 37

CHAPTER 14: *When My Bones Became Flesh through Faith*

Ezekiel 37:6, 1 Corinthians 15:58, Hebrews 6:10, 1 Thessalonians 1:3, 2 Corinthians 5:17, Philippians 4:13, Isaiah 55:11, Psalms 139:14, Genesis 30:13, Deuteronomy 28:1-14, Romans 4:20, Ezekiel 37:6-10

CHAPTER 15: *Turn Your Water into Wine*

John 2:1-11, John 10:27, Genesis 15, Numbers 23:19-20

CHAPTER 16: *When the Devil Steals Your Word of Faith*

Matthew 17:21, John 10:10, John 8:36, Romans 7:19-20, Matthew 17:14-21, Romans 10:17

CHAPTER 17: *When the Lord Calls Your Name say, "Here I am."*

Isaiah 58:9, Matthew 14:22-36, I Corinthians 1:27, Romans 2:11, I Samuel 1:5, Ecclesiastes 9:11, 2 Timothy 2:21, Psalms 139:14, Philippians 4:13

***** **FAITH SESSION 4** *****

CHAPTER 18: *You Shall Have What You Speak*

1 John 1:9, Romans 8:1, Joshua 23:14, Psalms 34:13, Proverbs 18:21, James 1:26, Proverbs 15:4

CHAPTER 19: *The Foundation Is Already Laid*

Hebrews 11:1, Matthew 17:20, Deuteronomy 28:1-14, Isaiah 45:3, Luke 6:38, Genesis 24:1-16, Jeremiah 29:11, Numbers 23:19-20

CHAPTER 20: *It's Your Appointed Season*

Deuteronomy 15:1-5, 2 Chronicles 20:1-26, 2 Chronicles 1:20

CHAPTER 21: *Stay Close to the Vine*

John 15:1-7, John 10:27, Genesis 2:5, 15

Share Your Success Story

> *I am positioning myself in these areas so that I can receive great success.*

My Notes and Extra Study

Position Your Faith for Great Success

Order Book Today!

When Ramona Got Her Groove Back From God

When Ramona Got Her Groove Back from God is a remarkable novel based on a woman's struggle for inner peace that is so poignantly portrayed in this dynamic, funny, unfettered, spiritual, story of betrayal and urban feigned love that was restored to spiritual love…

$16.00 *Paperback, plus S&H*
$24.95 *Hardback, plus S&H*

To order or order in bulk visit Heavenly Realm website,

heavenlyrealm@heavenlyrealmpublishing.comcastbiz.net
www.heavenlyrealmpublishing.net
or write to: stephanie2fr7@yahoo.com

Heavenly Realm Publishing
505 N. Sam Houston Pkwy. E., Suite 670
Houston, Texas 77060
Toll free: 1-877-599-3237

My Song of Solomon

"Many waters cannot quench love, neither can floods drown it..."
These were the words that Solomon Pierre' spoke softly to Barina Grant. She was petite with long kinky beautiful colored hair and had smooth light cream colored skin. While Solomon on the other hand, a poet with words and a spiritual love song in his heart; who had a deep and intriguing voice, a 6' foot stature, honey nut colored skin and muscles to be noticed. His words were ineffable. They were incapable of being expressed into words—they were just that breath taking. The thought of her ever finding true love was almost impossible as she became a 14-year old mother, and went from being homeless to a warehouse worker, to a prosperous writer. After meeting Solomon her feelings turned to him possibly being her eternal love. But through time and wrong choices, she nearly lost her life, her dreams, her career, and almost lost her mind. Yes will be the story that Barina will tell in this hope-filled, dynamic, moving, and purpose filled fiction story of feigned love, later turned into destined divine love...

$15.00 *Paperback, plus S&H*
$24.99 *Hardback, plus S&H*
or write to:
Heavenly Realm Publishing
505 N. Sam Houston Parkway E., Suite 670
Houston, Texas 77060
toll free: 1-877-599-3237
heavenlyrealm@heavenlyrealmpublishing.comcastbiz.net

My Song of Solomon *Prayer Journal*

My Song of Solomon *Prayer Journal*

$10.00 *plus S&H*

A prayer journal

To order, or order in bulk visit Heavenly Realm website.
or write to: stephanie2fr7@yahoo.com

Heavenly Realm Publishing
505 N. Sam Houston Pkwy. E., Suite 670
Houston, Texas 77060
Toll free: 1-877-599-3237
heavenlyrealm@heavenlyrealmpublishing.comcastbiz.net
www.heavenlyrealmpublishing.net

Position Your Faith for Great Success *Workbook*

Position Your Faith for Great Success Workbook

$17.00 *plus S&H*

A Workbook
To order, or order in bulk visit Heavenly Realm website.
or write to: stephanie2fr7@yahoo.com

Heavenly Realm Publishing Company
505 N. Sam Houston Pkwy. E., Suite 670
Houston, Texas 77060
Local: 1-281-999-3237
Toll free: 1-877-599-3237
heavenlyrealm@heavenlyrealmpublishing.comcastbiz.net

Position Your Faith for Great Success Workbook is packed with challenging questions from the book, "Position Your Faith for Great Success". It is also filled with a 7-day series of study, bible quizzes, faith scriptures, declarations, confirmations, and answers on faith, success, purpose, and promise.

This workbook will move you to reach for great success and learn how to have faith on how to move the heart of God even though you cannot see how your situation is going to work out.

Remember, it doesn't matter what mistakes you've made in the past, how you've been hurt, how you was not supported, not having the confidence to know that you can obtain great success, or maybe you just didn't know that you had a purpose to fulfill in this life. What ever your situation is, you can still have great success and know that you have the faith and the power to reach the unreachable, to do the impossible, out think the unthinkable, and see what has never been seen before. It's yours, go after it!

You're encouraged to purchase the book, "Position Your Faith for Great Success in order to successfully complete this workbook.

About the Author

She's the best-selling author of, "When Ramona Got Her Groove Back from God". She is also the author of My Song of Solomon, My Song of Solomon *Prayer Journal,* and Position Your Faith for Great Success Workbook. Stephanie is letting her multi-talents shine, but within all of these talents she's quick to give God all the glory. She is an author, playwright, director, producer, poet, designer, illustrator, motivational speaker, minister, entrepreneur, and educator. Evangelist Stephanie Franklin is all of these things and more. She speaks to the hearts of those who are in need of a life transformation and an up-lifting spiritual and mental move. God has called, anointed, and appointed her to be a Prophetess and to evangelize the world. She is very humble in allowing God to use her spiritual gifts in prophecy, healing, and deliverance. As a result, many people have been uplifted, healed, and delivered under her powerful prophetic ministry.

Her novels have so many twists and turns that will keep you on the edge of your seat and your eyes flowing through every line. Her spiritual realism, dazzling—heart turning and soul moving novels will make you want to change your life at a heart beat. Her books of faith, success, and purpose will turn your faith and determination towards a whole new dimension of, if you just have faith and confidence in yourself, you can do the impossible. Her work ministers to the hearts of millions all over the world, inspiring them to change, and challenging them to love and to live a new and wholesome life.

www.ingramcontent.com/pod-product-compliance
Lightning Source LLC
Chambersburg PA
CBHW031610160426
43196CB00006B/81